STANISLAVSKI IN REHEARSAL
The Final Years

by *Vasily Osipovich Toporkov*

translated by
Christine Edwards

Routledge
A Theatre Arts Book
New York and London

A Theatre Arts Book
published by Routledge
29 West 35th Street
New York, NY 10001

Translation © 1979 by Christine Edwards

Published by arrangement with Mme. Larissa Toporkova and
the U.S.S.R. Copyright Agency/VAAP

First published in paperback in 1998.

10 9 8 7 6 5 4 3 2 1

Library of Congress Cataloging-in-Publication Data

Toporkov, Vasilii Osipovich
    [K.S. Stanislavskiĭ na repetitsiĭ. English.]
    Stanislavski in rehearsal : the final years / by Vasilii Osipovich
    Toporkov : Translated by Christine Edwards.
        p.   cm.
    ISBN 0-87830-091-0 (pbk.)
    1. Stanislavsky, Konstantin, 1863–1938. 2. Method (Acting)
I. Title
PN278.S78T613   1998
792'. 028'092—dc21
                                                98-35554
                                                CIP

ACKNOWLEDGMENTS

I WISH TO EXPRESS my special gratitude and thanks to George Zournas, editor and publisher of Theatre Arts Books, for his painstaking care and generous help to me in editing this manuscript.

I am grateful to Leota Diesel, who died just as she finished preparing this manuscript for the printer, her mind filled with the noble words of Stanislavski, whom she had venerated for a lifetime.

I should like also to acknowledge my indebtedness to Vera Soloviova, former member of the Moscow Art Theatre, whose unique knowledge made her an indispensable aid to me in completing this translation; to Klaudia Petrovna Schreder, who came to my assistance in many moments of perplexity; to Toni Milford, whose faith in me has been a constant source of encouragement; and to three of my friends in Moscow: Larissa Toporkova, for first giving me permission to make this translation, Nina Mintz, who with Toporkova furnished me with many valuable items of information, and Vladimir Prokofiev, for first urging me to translate this book.

Finally, I want to offer my warm appreciation and deepest thanks to Helen Mamikonian, associate professor of Russian and French at Simmons College, Boston, for her priceless contribution in reading this translation and making many invaluable suggestions.

—CHRISTINE EDWARDS

K. S. Stanislavski

"One must not speak in dry scientific language with actors, and, in any case, I myself am not a man of science; I couldn't think of doing something out of my line.

"My task is to speak with the actor in his own language. Not to philosophize about art, but to reveal in simple form the practical methods of psychotechnique needed by him for the artistic embodiment of inner emotional experience."

—K. S. Stanislavski

FOREWORD

THIS BOOK WAS WRITTEN by one of the most outstanding actors of our day—People's Artist of the U.S.S.R. Vasily Osipovich Toporkov. Coming to the Moscow Art Theatre from the Korsh Theatre in Petersburg, by long and tenacious work he mastered the Stanislavski system, a new artistic technique which revealed great creative possibilities to him. His meeting with Stanislavski marked for Toporkov the beginning of a new life in art which compelled him to reexamine his theatre knowledge and views on the art of the actor.

In comparison with other artists of the Moscow Art Theatre whose creative life for decades had been in direct contact with Stanislavski and Nemirovich-Danchenko, Toporkov was associated with Stanislavski for a relatively short time, the last decade of Stanislavski's life. But for the very reason that Toporkov came to the Moscow Art Theatre after many years in other theatres, he was able to perceive sharply the contrast between the new ideas that Stanislavski taught and the usual teachings at the other theatres.

Toporkov became a passionate exponent of the teachings of Stanislavski. In his numerous talks with young people of the theatre, in his speeches and articles, he shared the creative experience of his work with Stanislavski.

The reminiscences of Toporkov are especially valuable because they are written by a direct participant in the last creative searches of Stanislavski. A man of great observation, of a sharp and inquisitive mind, Toporkov not only preserves

11

the remarks of his teacher which were made during rehearsals, not only reconstructs the atmosphere of the rehearsal process, but thoroughly reports Stanislavski's teaching methods. This book is not the memoirs of an actor, it is an important document which demonstrates the actual work of Konstantin Sergeyevich Stanislavski with the actor in creating a character. Toporkov's book, to a considerable extent, fills the gap which exists in our knowledge of Stanislavski's system. Stanislavski, who had written two volumes of *The Work of the Actor on Himself*° about the creative process of "emotional experience" and "embodiment," did not have time to complete the many volumes he had planned about the art of the actor. More than once Stanislavski pointed out that his system could be learned only through practice, so Toporkov here describes the actual work of Stanislavski's last years (1927–38). This book is at present the only source which fully describes Stanislavski's method of creating an actor's technique, a method which he applied in the work on *Dead Souls* and, especially, on *Tartuffe*, which he considered his "artistic testament."

Like Stanislavski, who in *My Life in Art* wrote about his achievements and successes, but chiefly about his searches and failures, Toporkov, who was one of Stanislavski's favorite actors, recounts principally his mistakes while leaving in shadow his acting triumphs. One of the most popular actors in Moscow, upon joining the Moscow Art Theatre, he bravely renounced his success with the public for the sake of learning from Stanislavski how to master the laws of an actor's creativity. According to his own account, the work with Konstantin Sergeyevich on the role of Chichikov in the play *Dead Souls* was the most important step of his artistic life. "I followed a difficult path," Toporkov recounts, "I suffered a great deal, experienced many shocks, failures, and disappointments; but nothing weakened my faith in the correctness of the way shown me by Stanislavski." The great director led him finally

---

° Published in English as *An Actor Prepares, Building a Character* and *Creating a Role*.

to that path "in search of which I had had to wander long and agonizingly in the darkness." This path brought him to the laws of organic creativity which opened the door to further progress.

Toporkov did not succeed at once in the difficult role of Chichikov. But after a series of performances he began to play the essence of the character, bringing to life Chichikov's style and sharp, meaty humor. What was outstanding in the characterizations of Toporkov was the fervor, the inner involvement, the delicacy of the psychological pattern, the great naturalness and credibility with, at the same time, the most exact stage expressiveness. Both Chichikov and Molière's Orgon, as well as many other roles, were played by him with real inspiration and temperament. He established a new interpretation of Molière which gave rise to enthusiastic praise from all sides and can be reckoned among the highest achievements of the Moscow Art Theatre. Toporkov owed his greatest success as an actor, for the most part, to the directorial-pedagogical genius of Stanislavski. The Stanislavski system does not create talent, but the talented actor, armed with the system, discovers new sources of creativity in himself which make possible the maximum development of those talents."

For anyone who was at the rehearsals of Konstantin Sergeyevich, the intense searching, as accepted ideas were destroyed and completely new creative horizons and tasks were revealed, was memorable. "This unusual person had unusual power over me.... He awakened the artist in me.... He showed me artistic perspectives of which I had never dreamed, and which would never have unfolded before me without him," wrote Vasily Kachalov about Stanislavski in those years when the enemies of the Art Theatre spoke against the directorial "despotism" of Stanislavski.

Striving to free the actor from routine playing and to bring him close to creativity, attempting to free his individuality from the shackling clichés and theatrical conventions which prevent him from feeling himself a living person who can live the organic life of the role, Stanislavski was uncompromising in his demands, persistently repudiating the path of compromise. He was a perfectionist. In the words of an actor of the Moscow Art Theatre, "working with him was torture and joy, but more often torture until you understood the way by which he led and lured the actor to the desired goal." He wanted to obtain simple, clear, logically consistent, organic behavior from the actor, he wanted a complete merging of the actor with the role. But those seemingly simple tasks turned out to be difficult to fulfill, since they demanded of the actors perfect artistic technique and that absolute sincerity which leads to complete artistic embodiment.

In his striving for that noble, artistic simplicity which is the result of high mastery, artistic taste, and a very special technique, Stanislavski regarded impatiently everything false, everything artificially "theatrical," which cripples the actor, which hinders him, and delays his creative growth. He drew a sharp line between art and hack work; he hated dilettantism, routine acting, overplaying, self-satisfaction. He mercilessly destroyed all that makes up what he called "the cursed actor's trade."

True to the precepts of Mikhail Shchepkin, Stanislavski demanded from the actor systematic and persistent work toward self-perfection throughout the course of the actor's life. Working with Stanislavski, who had the highest aims in art, was no easy matter. But those who went through his severe schooling, who had, in the words of Toporkov, withstood "this trial by fire," came out changed, tempered; they had experienced the utmost creative joy. "Believe me, all the things which now seem to you so difficult, are in reality nothing but trifles. Have the patience to examine, to think over and understand these trifles, and you will know better the joys which are within a man's reach in this world," wrote Stanislavski to Knipper-Chekhova, who was confused and disturbed by his new method when it was applied for the first time in rehearsals of *A Month in the Country*. "I beg you to be staunch and valiant in this artistic struggle which you have to win," he wrote her, "not only for the sake of your talent, which I love with all my heart, but also for the sake of our entire theatre, which is the meaning of my whole life. . . ." It was so in the first years of the application of the system, when Stanislavski demanded that the actors of the Art Theatre, who had already formed their methods of playing, "learn anew from the beginning," and it was so in the last years of Stanislavski's life, of which Toporkov here writes with such emotion and fidelity. Konstantin Sergeyevich used to say to the participants in the experimental work on *Tartuffe*, "Remember that every great actor who is exacting, after a certain span of time—say four or five years—must go back to 'school' again." It is significant that among the group of actors of the Moscow Art Theatre who came to Stanislavski's studio to learn more perfect methods of artistic technique, along with Kedrov, Toporkov, Koreneva, and other artists, there were also the famous old masters of the Theatre: Knipper-Chekhova and Leonidov.

The continuation of the art of the Moscow Art Theatre worried Stanislavski as well as Nemirovich-Danchenko. It was an art that demanded continual renewal and perfection. They considered that it was founded on "the reproduction and transmission of organic life," which does not allow static forms and traditions, however beautiful. It was alive and, like all that exists, was in continuous movement and development: Stanislavski didn't look on his system as something once and forever established and completed.

In his work on *Tartuffe*, Stanislavski for the first time applied a new method which received the name "the method of physical actions." Kedrov, who carried out the production of *Tartuffe* after Stanislavski's death, and in his further work at the Moscow Art Theatre continued the method of physical actions and instilled it in the practice of the theatre, maintained that "this method brings great concreteness to the work of the actor. It is based on the indivisible unity of the physical and spiritual life of a person and is built on the correct organization of the physical line of the actor's life on the stage. The purpose of this method is to penetrate, through the logical and correct fulfillment of physical actions, into those complicated, deep feelings and emotional experiences which the actor must call out of himself in order to create the given stage image."

Toporkov's book, in which the whole process of the creation of *Tartuffe* is depicted so clearly and in such detail, will help to clarify this method of physical actions to which Stanislavski, in his last years, gave such decisive value. By concrete, clear examples, Toporkov shows that "physical action," as Stanislavski understood it, is by no means simple physical movement, but is in essence psychophysical action which includes the psychological task. "There is no physical action without volition, without objectives and problems, and without inner justification of them by one's feelings; there is no invention or product of the imagination which does not demand one action or another; there must not be on the stage physical actions without genuineness or without the sensation of truth . . ." wrote Stanislavski, who asserted that "all this bears witness to the close bond of physical action with all the inner elements of the actor's feelings."

The search for those consecutive, logical physical actions which bring the actor to the sensation of truth, in the search for which Stanislavski worked so long and persistently with the actors in rehearsals, might seem to the casual and superficial observer only exercises in technique, without any direct relation to the work on the discovery of the ideas of a play. But, in essence, for Stanislavski questions of technique were not isolated from the ideas and general aims of the play. Konstantin Sergeyevich repeatedly and persistently emphasized the fact that the primary role in creativity is the idea of the play. Rejecting dry rationality and artificial "creativity," Stanislavski in the first volume of *The Actor's Work on Himself (An Actor Prepares)* clearly shows the necessity for the consciously supplied superobjective, which is found by analyzing the production and discovering the idea underlying it.

Stanislavski demanded a *conscious* superobjective which comes from an interesting creative idea; he insisted that the incarnate superobjective be continuous, uninterrupted, passing through the whole role and the whole play. "The first concern of the actor is not to lose sight of the superobjective," wrote Stanislavski. "To forget about this means to break the lifeline of the play. This is a castastrophe for the role, for the actor and for the play." The means of discovering the superobjective and the through-line-of-action was considered by Stanislavski to be the chief contribution of his system.

Toporkov clearly shows how Stanislavski always strove his utmost to reveal the content of each episode, of each scene. From the actors he sought a truthful, logical, consistent, and continuous action which was complete, with its own inner logic and development and which was filled with the sharpest rhythms; he sought an action which clearly expressed the inner meaning of each scene and the central task which defined the behavior of each character.

In contrast to the popularizers of his teaching who try to isolate the method of physical actions and the other elements of his system, Stanislavski saw them not as ends in themselves but as auxiliaries which help the actor go from the simple to the complicated, from simple physical actions to complex psychological emotional experiences, as helps toward the creation of the character and the discovery of the ideological conflict of the production.

Stanislavski's system continues and develops the basic principles of Russian esthetic thought. In his fundamental theoretical position Stanislavski took his inspiration from the remarkable statements of Pushkin, Gogol, and Shchepkin about stage art. The thoughts of Belinsky about the high socioeducational purposes of the theatre and about the distinctive character of Russian realistic art were dear to him, as was the precept of Chernishevski—"Beauty is life." The creative ideas of Gorky and Chekhov also enriched his system, which is a deep and wise application of the genuine traditions of Russian artistic culture.

From its beginning, Stanislavski's system was in an uncompromising struggle with all those theories of theatrical decadence which hid under false, pseudo-revolutionary phrases. "There are false searches and schools which seem, temporarily, to threaten the foundations of high realistic art, but they have not the strength to destroy it completely," said Stanislavski.

When the work on *Dead Souls* was in full swing, he learned of the ill-fated production of *Hamlet* at the theatre of Eugene Vakhtangov, where the director perverted Shakespeare, turning that great philosophical tragedy into a parody, a farce—gleefully mocking a fat Hamlet occupied with a struggle for the throne and picturing Ophelia as a girl of light reputation. Stanislavski was filled with indignation and bitterness. On that day, Toporkov recalls, Stanislavski, in class, "made unrealistic demands on us, angrily attacking us for the slightest blunder or display of bad taste. That day he was at times cruel and unjust. We were paying for those who had outraged the genius of Shakespeare."

"Hot arguments often arise over Stanislavski's system; there are many different interpretations of it. That is understandable because it literally touches upon all questions of the actor's creativity and mastery. Its spirit of continual, tireless striving, that spirit which nourished the genius of Stanislavski, is especially precious. The system is, for us, an excellent directive to action, not a dogmatic compendium of fixed standards and truth," wrote Kedrov, who stood at the head of the artistic leadership of the Moscow Art Theatre.

Toporkov here receates for us the noble, majestic image of Stanislavski, an artist of genius, a teacher and warrior, whose creative legacy enriches our art. Toporkov's book is not only for practical workers in the theatre, critics and historians of the theatre and students of the theatre, it is for all who are interested in creativity and the art of the stage.

From an article by N. Chushkin

Stanislavski in Rehearsal

Vasily Osipovich Toporkov as CHICHIKOV

PREFACE

AFTER GRADUATING FROM the Petersburg Imperial Theatre School in 1909, in my twentieth year, full of confidence in myself, in my power, knowledge, and technical readiness, I boldly began to walk the difficult road of the actor and in my first steps . . . stumbled.

My naïve, youthful stage babble was at once lost in the sea of confident professionalism of my new colleagues, whose company I entered upon graduation from the theatre school. From that time there started a continuous cycle of hope and grief which often brought me to despair, a state which is known to every person who devotes himself to the stage.

In our art there is a lack of any exact knowledge, of any theoretical basis. This is a phenomenon peculiar to the theatre and it is considered by many quite natural, but it contributes to agonizing creative crises.

Stanislavski, by illuminating many obscure aspects of the creative process, delivered us from wandering along uncertain paths and showed us the most secure and true road to mastery.

I was fortunate to work under his direct leadership.

In educating the actor, Stanislavski not only equipped him with a professional technique but also developed him spiritually, directing him to the path of service to art.

"We must love not ourself in art, but art in ourself," he used to say.

And this art, armed with a most encompassing artistic technique and directed toward the lofty goal of the education of the people, was always Stanislavski's ideal.

The great authority of Stanislavski, his exhaustive knowledge of the creative nature of the actor, gave him the right to conduct bold experiments with actors. The great demands imposed by him upon them led, in the last analysis, to simpler, clearer solutions to the problems of the embodiment of a role.

Honoring the memory of this great teacher, counting myself eternally indebted to him, I have decided to write of those last creative meetings with this genius, to tell of the new ways he found to create a role and a production, and in this way to make the path toward the comprehension of the Stanislavski system easier.

V.O. Toporkov

THE START
OF THE ROAD

IN MY LIFE I went through two schools of acting: the first was the Petersburg Imperial Theatre School at the Alexandrinsky Theatre (1906–9) and the second was the practical work with Stanislavski at the Moscow Art Theatre (1927–38).

Looking back to my first schooling and comparing it with the school of Stanislavski, I come more and more to the conviction that graduating from the best Petersburg school, with all its merits, was, all the same, for me little more than getting a diploma, while my studies with Stanislavski made it possible for me to appreciate the true foundations of our art.

In this connection, it is of interest to recall the circumstances in our theatrical schools before Stanislavski discovered his system. For me this is not so difficult to do since I myself, as I said before, learned about theatre art in a "pre-Stanislavski" school, at a time when Konstantin Sergeyevich was only beginning his experiments, when he did not yet have much authority, especially with us in Petersburg.

The most influential teacher at the Imperial Theatre School in Petersburg was the famous artist of the Alexandrinsky Theatre, V. N. Davydov. He was the white-haired patriarch of the school, its indisputable authority. To be one of his pupils was considered great good luck; they adored him and obeyed him implicitly. During the lessons there was perfect discipline. Several times I was present at those lessons and was asked to rehearse with his students. At these times he impressed me a great deal, and his lessons were extremely interesting in their own way.

As soon as he entered the rehearsal hall, young actors would surround Davydov, who would carry on conversations with them about the theatre, about great Russian actors and the outstanding Italian tragedian Tommaso Salvini, whom he valued and very cleverly imitated. Then he would turn to the play which they had to rehearse; he would tell each actor where he was not succeeding and where he was; he would speak about the play and about each role separately. Everything was very convincing, clear, understandable. The students would run to the stage, begin to rehearse, and immediately find out that ideas which seemed so simple, clear and easily attainable were not so at all. Their weak technique was not able to master even the hundredth part of what had been explained so vividly by their teacher. And the more brilliant his account, the more helpless and worthless they felt. From the stage came boredom, colorlessness and hopelessness. The great master either fell asleep under the monotonous recitation of his pupils, who were playing a gay comedy, or burst with indignation and scolded each player, making killing caricatures of his acting. Then, notwithstanding his advanced years and obesity, in a youthful manner he would run to the stage, brilliantly play all the roles himself, and, pleased with the applause of his brood, leave the stage to sit down in an armchair with a gleeful exclamation: "Was that me or the Devil?"

Soothed by his own success, Davydov would get into a pleasant mood and finish the lesson with joyful stories or demonstrations of card tricks or juggling, which he performed brilliantly. He urged his pupils learn the art of juggling and magic: "An actor should be able to do everything; in addition to acting, he must be able to sing, dance, and do magic tricks."

The charm of that great artist, his penetrating, persuasive statements, the demonstrations of his own skill, the paternal concern for his pupils, which extended beyond the walls of the school, all taken together, could not but have an enormous influence upon those future actors. The great Shchepkin tradition of realistic art, which blossomed at that time in the theatre, was implanted in the theatrical schools by such teachers as Davydov. His pupils, under his influence, acquired an artistic appearance which distinguished them from the provincial, self-taught actor.

Other teachers of this time had their own individual peculiarities, their own skill in the instruction and education of young actors, but there was one general quality common to all: the absence of a firm theatrical basis and an orderly pedagogical system of education. That which passed for "system" with them did not approach what later on was made concrete by Stanislavski.

I had studied in Petersburg and knew only the teachers of that city. Perhaps in Moscow the state of affairs was different. I had never been to Moscow; I had not attended classes of the prominent Moscow teachers A. P. Lensky, M. P. Sadovsky, and others. But what I heard from their pupils, who referred to them with great respect, showed that matters there stood approximately the same as in Petersburg.

There is no doubt that Lensky and Davydov taught a whole line of actors of whom we are truly proud; it could not be otherwise. However, the subsequent development of our art demanded, in turn, further improvements of the teaching system. Stanislavski succeeded in uncovering many secrets of artistic technique which our great artists possessed but yet could not explain sufficiently to their pupils, although they strove to do so with all their hearts.

S. Yakovlev, an artist of the Alexandrinsky Theatre in whose class I finished at the theatre school, distinguished himself somewhat in this respect from his colleagues. Having completed his studies under Davydov, he went to Moscow and studied with A. F. Fedotov. When he returned to Petersburg, he brought ideas about teaching acting which were new for that time.

By comparison with Davydov, Yakovlev's method of teaching was more progressive, and in his classes there was a different atmosphere, which was apparent to me as I was working at the same time in Davydov's class. There was also a period when, because of the illness of Yakovlev, Davydov conducted classes for his former student. We young people, in spite of all our respect and admiration for Davydov, regarded his old methods somewhat critically.

In what way was this relative progressiveness of Yakovlev expressed? At that time the art of declamation flourished—there were even recitations to music—and in the school they made use of this. In the first half of the school year, together with basic subjects, the pupils were taught elocutionary art, which bore no direct relation to the art of stage acting. About this, they understood little, and three quarters of a year was spent in studies which were useless and, to some degree, even harmful to our art. Very often the successful student-declaimer, as soon as he passed on to work in dramatic art, found himself unready for it.

To these studies of the first year Yakovlev brought essential changes, giving them a more expedient and correct direction. At the very first lesson he defined the difference between reading and acting. He never even mentioned declamation and he had no intention of teaching it to us. For the reading of literary fragments, he conceived special ways of speaking more colloquially. I will not be specific here about those exercises in verbal action because later on we will meet with them many times. While the studies with Yakovlev proceeded along this channel, everything went well and the pupils developed as they took their first correct steps. But sometimes after the reading of excerpts, Yakovlev would suddenly stop this necessary and useful training and continue along a completely wrong road.

Because he was an actor of spontaneous temperament and deep emotional experience, it was in that way he regarded our art and when approaching questions of emotion in these studies, he was particularly demanding of his pupils. But that which came easily to the highly talented Yakovlev was not so simple for his pupils. It was evident that he never had to think from where his temperament came, how the characters created by him were filled with feeling; he did not need a "pole in order to jump," he had only to visualize a thing in order to bring about the desired result. It was not so for his twenty pupils, each having his own individuality, special temperament, mentality and habits. Yakovlev did not yet know how to awaken real feelings in the actor, live, organic temperament; he did not know those gates, which were later found by Stanislavski, through which one can truthfully arrive at the desired goal.

Yakovlev turned from the right path on which the first half year of his teaching was founded and stepped onto the forbidden path of forcing the feelings. Having finished work with the descriptive literary fragments, Yakovlev gave his pupils special emotion-filled literary works or monologues such as "On the Death of a Poet" by Lermontov, the final monologue of Chatsky, the monologue of Dmitri, the false Tsar in *Boris Godunov,* or something of that kind. He demanded that the reading be filled with great temperament, with deep feeling. However, he did not give us any real help in this and he would not accept any excuses if the desired effect was not achieved; then it was, in his expression, "blah, blah, blah."

"Stepan Ivanovich, I am not in the mood today. I cannot call forth any feelings. . . ."

"That doesn't concern me," he would answer. "Feelings should be . . . read this poem with flowing tears."

"But I have none!"

"Go borrow from Volkov-Semenov" (as the library was called where we borrowed the plays).

Yakovlev had no doubt that, above all, the actor had to have temperament, had to have feelings, and if he did not have them at a given moment, then the actor had to "pump" himself, repeating again and again the scene or poem in which he had failed. He even had a special way of encouraging an actor by tapping his foot on the floor during the rehearsal, in order not to interrupt the rendition. It would have been better to interrupt the actor who was "tearing a passion to pieces," calm him down and encourage him to use those elements of stage technique, including the creation of images, which Stanislavski used for uncovering real, live feelings in a student.

Following the road indicated by Yakovlev, his pupils, together and individually, trustfully practiced the development of their temperament, shouting in fury in all keys such heroic phrases as: "You are my witness, Almighty God!" "Oh, you hypocrite!" "No, this is much too much!" "You lie, Rabbi!," etc. The young pupils, alas, saw with their inner eye not the character or image contained in these sentences, but their ideal, Stepan Ivanovich, stamping his foot with emotion.

Yakovlev made one of his favorite students, one possessing great gifts, read at each lesson over the course of three years the monologue of Joan of Arc in Schiller's *Maid of Orleans*, trying to awaken a heroic temperament in her. But neither the brilliant story of how Yermolova used to play the role, how she delivered this monologue, nor his endless tapping of the floor helped. The temperament of the young actress did not awaken, and, although sometimes there were sparks, they did not come as the result of Yakovlev's method but in spite of it. To fix the feeling which flashed out once was impossible: it had departed as unexpectedly as it had appeared. To bring out real feelings it was necessary to use much more reliable methods. These, unfortunately, Yakovlev did not know.

Working on plays, Yakovlev vacillated between true and false teaching methods. He renounced the method of demonstrating how to play this or that role or scene, and he steadfastly adhered to this principle; he never once went out upon the stage for a visual demonstration to his pupils, as his teacher Davydov often used to do. And it is also true that, although somewhat vaguely, all the same he appreciated the value of simple physical actions on the stage and directed our attention to them; nevertheless, he had no conception of Stanislavski's method of using them.

However, he used to say, "Once you portray real life, then everything that you do on the stage—if you drink tea, if you peel potatoes and so on—must correspond to it." Although Yakovlev cannot be accused of leading his students to the portrayal of just the outer image, he did lead them away from the path which Stanislavski used: to proceed first of all from one's human nature, from one's own feelings, to the manifestation peculiar to the actor in the given circumstances of a play.

Yakovlev, while speaking of correct procedures, as noted above, and while employing them to some degree in practice, at the same time contradicted himself by stressing an unnecessary pragmatism.

"I am making actors of you. . . . The majority of you will have to go to work in the provinces. There you will have to prepare a role in two or three rehearsals. You must be ready for this. Therefore, above everything, practice. We will learn how to prepare a new production in two weeks. When you finish school, you will have skill and a repertoire."

Skill for what? For hack work. But to some extent Yakovlev was right. How many students, having finished school, succeeded in getting jobs in the theatres of the capital? The situation in the provincial theatre was such that they needed actors with a large repertory who could work fast and adapt themselves quickly to any conditions.

In the schools the course of study in acting was usually planned for three years, and this was considered enough preparation for a young actor. All hopes for the further perfecting of his skills were pinned on practical work in the professional theatre. Such a view was due to a limited knowledge of acting technique.

But while speaking of the shortcomings of the old teaching, I by no means want to belittle either the great meaning which the theatre schools of that time had for the growth of our stage culture, or, even less, discredit their teachers, those great artists of the Russian theatre. Many artists, outstanding ones such as V. N. Davydov, Y. M. Yuryev, A. P. Petrovsky, Y. E. Ozarovsky, A. A. Sanin and, finally, my teacher, S. I. Yakovlev, each in his own way contributed to the great work of educating the actor.

They all recognized the importance of the theatrical schools, loved them and gave them their support without any mercenary motive. They did not receive any special sympathy from the majority of the actors of the time, who were scornful of such schools. I draw attention to their imperfections only in order to define more exactly the truly gigantic leap which was made by the genius of Stanislavski.

Directing at that time was only beginning its timid attempts to change from simple stage management to creative teaching.

Yuri M. Yuryev describes in his memoirs a case where Davydov, while rehearsing Ostrovsky's *The Ardent Heart*, broke rehearsal tradition by interrupting the flow of a rehearsal which had already begun. The scene was not coming out right, and Davydov, trying to get the necessary result, again and again requested that it be repeated; this called forth a murmur of indignation among the players. "This is not a school," they told him. And this was said to an artist who enjoyed great authority in the company, one who was the pride of the Russian stage! What could an ordinary director do, who found himself among such a crowd of "great artists"?

At that time they had begun to talk about the "eccentricities" of the director Stanislavski at the Art Theatre. The rumors were contradictory and unclear: now they said that Stanislavski was turning the artists into marionettes who carried out his despotic will, or into performing monkeys who did everything according to the instructions of their trainer; at other times, on the contrary, they said that Stanislavski, while rehearsing, sometimes demanded improvisations of the actors, not showing them either the exact mise en scène or doing anything that was usual in conducting a rehearsal. Suddenly the unbelievable rumor was spread that Stanislavski, working with the actor I. M. Uralov on the role of the governor in *The Inspector General*, rehearsed a scene with him, "The Governor in the Bazaar," which was neither in the play nor in any of the author's rough drafts!

Actors of the Moscow Art Theatre, who now and then would appear in the company of actors of other theatres, were already flaunting their special understanding of art, their knowledge of some kind of mysterious terminology, their special approach to the work on a role. These bold novelties broke with old theatre traditions and the "extravagances" of Stanislavski called forth sharp rebuffs from leading figures of the Alexandrinsky Theatre.

An interesting episode comes to my mind. Uralov moved from the Art Theatre to the Alexandrinsky Theatre in Petersburg. Since he had played the governor in *The Inspector General* in Moscow, he was asked to alternate with Davydov in this role at the Alexandrinsky Theatre. Once during a break in the rehearsal Uralov respectfully addressed Davydov with a question about creativity and the following dialogue took place:

"Tell me, Vladimir Nikolaevich, in the first act, with what do you come in to the official?"

"What is this 'with what'?" countered Davydov, as if not understanding.

"Well, with what feeling, with what intention. . . . Here we are told that he . . ." (There followed a long explanation of the different tasks, given circumstances, etc.)

Davydov, restraining his anger and contempt, listened attentively for some time and then interrupted Uralov with words full of sarcasm:

"I don't know 'with what' you come out at the Moscow Art Theatre, but I come out on the Imperial stage to play Gogol, and *I* come out, *I*, Vladimir Nikolaevich Davydov."

And, turning away, he let it be understood that the conversation was ended.

Of course he said that in a state of hot temper and irritation with a clever man who wished to be cleverer than a celebrated master. Davydov had a well-deserved reputation not only as a talented actor, but also as an artist who could reflect on, who could analyze a role, and with his fine understanding, create a well-rounded, magnificent character. And, in truth, on his entrance in the first scene of *The Inspector General* you could not feel even a shade of the conceit with which he spoke to Uralov. On the contrary, the appearance of Davydov struck us all with the fine, expressive logic of behavior of an alarmed functionary, worried about unpleasant events in his official life. One had to look at him only once to be able to say exactly "with what" the governor entered. By what road that great artist had come to such brilliant results remained a secret. It was to this "secret" that the searching eye of Stanislavski was turned.

The rumors about the work of Stanislavski at the Moscow Art Theatre which flew to Petersburg interested me, as well as others, at first only because the work seemed unusual, curious. But later, on reflecting and carefully analyzing the positions advanced by Stanislavski, I felt that in it all, undoubtedly, some grains of truth were hidden.

The Moscow Art Theatre was enjoying great fame at home and it also had ardent admirers in Petersburg, so it was only with the most incredible difficulty that I could obtain a ticket for one of its productions during its Petersburg guest tour. For a long time there had been passionate arguments about the young theatre. The professional actors of Petersburg, especially the venerable artists of the Imperial Theatre, did not at all accept the impudent innovations and eccentricities of the Art Theatre's Director/Producer Stanislavski. In fact, they considered his company, which consisted for the most part of young people from the Philharmonic Insitute and amateur acting societies, mere dilettantes—as indeed, they did Stanislavski himself—and predicted the imminent demise of such an unprofessional enterprise.

The Petersburg journal *Theatre and Art,* published by the renowned critic A. Kugel, was the leader of the opponents of the Art Theatre. In its pages, Kugel published crushing articles denouncing the new directions being taken in the art of the theatre, attacking the "anti-theatrical" repertoire of the Moscow Art Theatre and its absurd interpretations of plays. The articles emphasized the lack of experience of its actors.

It is not surprising then that I, a true Petersburger and a student at the Imperial Theatre School, although not yet having seen a single performance by the Moscow Art Theatre, was entirely on the side of its detractors. In talking with my friends about it, I parroted the words of my teachers Davydov and Yakovlev about "violations of tradition," "killing lively talent," "substituting 'creative work' for training," etc. But we were most scandalized by their completely preposterous, incomprehensibly exaggerated rehearsal periods.

Could my adored Alexandrists be wrong? Could such a critic as Kugel be mistaken? At that time I didn't even bother to pose such questions—I had no doubt that my idols were correct. But my desire to bolster my arguments with concrete facts spurred my efforts to get a ticket to the visitors' performances.

At last I had a ticket in my hand, and to their notorious production of *The Cherry Orchard* at that. The play was being done at the same time at the Alexandrinsky Theatre so I would be able to see both productions and compare.

Half an hour before curtain time, I entered the Mikhaelovski Theatre and noticed a sign that read: "Once the performance has begun, entrance into the theatre is forbidden." Lord, what strong measures!

Looking down from the loge to the packed orchestra, I noticed that the audience was not the kind that usually went to premieres at the Imperial Theatre, not the showy kind, that is, glittering with diamonds. No, in the theatre tonight were most of the Petersburg intelligentsia: writers, lawyers, doctors and artists. In the top balcony were the young people, the students. The theatre was buzzing with excitement like an alarmed beehive. In the orchestra and loges I recognized now one, now another famous person. I wanted to see everything, to remember everything. Suddenly, the lights in the chandeliers slowly began to dim and the hum began to subside as the walls of the theatre seemed to float away with my thoughts. . . .

As a ray of light cut through the darkness and illuminated the Moscow Art Theatre's emblem, a white seagull, on the huge gray curtain, I was aware that the theatre was in complete silence—all attention focused on that bright spot. The curtain slowly parted and there was the nursery of Ranevskaya's house.

I recognized immediately that it was a room in a venerable house; however, I felt that I was not in a theatre, but was looking into a room which was not my own but one with which I was vaguely familiar. For some reason I knew this nursery in Ranevskaya's house. It was in semidarkness, it was empty, nothing was happening—never mind, I involuntarily smiled in recognition. There was complete silence in the theatre; like me, everyone else was gazing at the set attentively, recognizing . . .

I continued to look, as if spellbound, afraid to move, anticipating something—but what? "It is true, no one should be admitted into the theatre just now," flashed into my mind. Suddenly, somewhere far away, a locomotive whistled and the maid Dunyasha, a candle in hand, ran into the room and looked through the window at the sunrise, while from the other room a sleepy Lopakhin entered. They began to talk. "But those are not actors! They are real people." Was that good or bad? I didn't have time to decide. Involuntarily I was drawn into their anxieties and, with them, waited with impatience for Ranevskaya's arrival. Finally, in the distance, the sound of sleigh bells was heard and Lopakhin and Dunyasha ran out to welcome. . . .

The stage is once again empty. But I greedily listen to the

sounds filtering through the windows; in response to them, I imagine the scene of the lady's arrival—the exclamations, the kisses, the laughter. The luggage is unloaded, there is a squabble among the peasants, the coachman shouts, the horses neigh, the bells ... everything is so interesting, so real, so familiar—a happy homecoming in the chill of the morning. One could listen to this, as to a good symphony, forever, but after a while the desire arises to see these people for oneself, and, strangely enough, as soon as the desire occurs, they all burst into the room with excited faces and impetuous movements. Everyone has his own concerns, his own affairs. At first I felt lost, I didn't know whom to watch, but gradually my attention came to rest on a tall man in an overcoat. I recognized him, it was Gaev.

The tall man, as he entered, seemed to bring with him life itself. What I saw seemed a miracle! How could a person, on the stage in front of a thousand people, be so completely occupied with his own cares? It did not occur to me immediately that this was Stanislavski himself. It didn't seem possible that I was seeing on the stage an actor and not that unlucky country gentleman Gaev. Stanislavski, the actor, didn't "astonish" me in any way; he didn't use the usual "big guns" in the actor's arsenal. I couldn't determine if, from an actor's point of view, that was good, but I simply couldn't take my eyes off him; it was as if he had bewitched me.

Throughout the evening I greedily absorbed everything that happened in that house. Everything was done naturally, with the utmost simplicty—as it should be. There was nothing invented, people actually live in this way, they act in this way, they suffer and are happy. Nothing done for show, nothing was "theatrical," but everything sank deep into the soul.

Perhaps the critics are right, one cannot "act" this way, these people are not "actors"—but why is our attention riveted on the stage? Why does all this excite us so?

That night, after the performance, I couldn't fall asleep for a long time. In the morning, I awoke troubled. Fragments of memories flashed into my head, but they were not memories of the actors or the spectacle of the performance—they were memories of the people of the cherry orchard and their fate. I pondered for a long time the lives of those people with whom, it seemed, I had become intimate. I wasn't concerned with whether Chekhov's play was "good" or not, whether the decor and staging were satisfactory, or how the actors had played. I couldn't explain it, but something had begun to stir deep in my consciousness—a reorientation, a new understanding of the possibilities of our art.

I was won over by their remarkable art which so clearly emphasized the obsoleteness of many traditions of my former idol—the Alexandrinsky Theatre. The gathering together there into a mighty group of the best representatives of the State Theatre—Davydov, Dalmatov, Varlamov, Michurina, Yakovlev—in *The Cherry Orchard* could not compete with the harmonious ensemble of their Moscow counterparts, which did not shine with such illustrious names, but was guided by the single will of its director-innovator.

That performance decided my fate. All my thoughts turned toward the new theatre, toward the new art; I began to search for ways of coming close to Stanislavski. My dream was realized only after twenty years. But this long wait was not fruitless. I worked a lot in the capital as well as in the provincial theatres, playing many roles, acquiring a great deal of experience. I had success, especially in the last period in the Korsh Theatre. Before I joined the Moscow Art Theatre I learned a lot, meeting many talented, experienced actors and directors. All that could serve as material for my memoirs, but I abandon that and proceed to the theme of the present book.

MY ENTRANCE INTO THE MOSCOW ART THEATRE

The Embezzlers

THE EDUCATION OF the actor in the Moscow Art Theatre technique demanded long and persistent work, but it also provided full protection for the student-actor from dangerous influences on the outside. Actors, in the words of Konstantin Sergeyevich, must be raised within the theatre; that is why the instances of inviting actors from outside to the Art Theatre were so few. My invitation was one of the rare exceptions.

As I have already said, I joined the Moscow Art Theatre group after almost twenty years' experience in acting. Up to that time, Stanislavski had not once seen me either on the stage or in life, and decided to invite me to the Theatre only at the urgent recommendation of persons who at that time, along with himself, managed the theatre and whom he trusted greatly. But all the same, the final decision on this question was long delayed; the acceptance of an actor into the Art Theatre was considered by Konstantin Sergeyevich an extremely important matter.

Hints about the forthcoming invitation to the Moscow Art Theatre were made about two years before I actually was invited. Stanislavski was analyzing this question from all sides, gathering information in different places and from different

37

people about everything that concerned me, not only as an actor but also as a person, a family man and a member of society. Finally, when my meeting with him took place in his official study, both of us were so excited that in our embarrassment we both tried to sit in the same chair. I felt his piercing gaze upon me, the look of an art collector who is buying a new article for his collection and is afraid of making a mistake.

Questions of inculcating and assimilating new acting techniques occupied Stanislavski to such an extent that they began to prevail over everything else, especially during the last years of his life. For this reason the attempt to reeducate an actor from another theatre in his method, naturally, held special interest for him. I, who had long dreamed of this meeting with the great master, was eager to absorb at firsthand all that which I, on so many occasions, had heard by word-of-mouth in theatrical circles, but which still remained not very clear. It was in such circumstances that I came into contact with Konstantin Sergeyevich in work which was to progress with unflagging interest on the part of us both.

My second meeting with Konstantin Sergeyevich took place in the study of his house in Leontyev Lane, where I, and every other actor who crossed its threshold, lived through so much excitement, joy, fear, desperation and hope.

This second meeting lasted quite a long time—three or four hours—and took place in cozy surroundings, which evidently had been prepared especially for the meeting with me: the table was set with bowls of nuts, sweets and fruits, which Konstantin Sergeyevich offered me. The conversation was, of course, about the theatre. He carefully drew from me information about my tastes. Which role, of all I had played, pleased me the most and why? What would I like to play? What did I like best of all that was now playing at the Moscow Art Theatre and at the other theatres? The whole range of questions which in our day, following his example, every director would ask when taking a new actor into his company. But at that time, this was a novelty and these questions, their great number and the care with which Konstantin Sergeyevich strove to get exhaustive answers, made a great impression on me.

The conversation was very interesting and instructive. But, unfortunately, my state of excitement prevented me from writing down our conversation in detail immediately afterward, and now, after so many years, it is difficult to reconstruct it. I will say only that the behavior of Konstantin Sergeyevich impressed me very much. His unlimited interest in all that touched the theatre struck me most of all. Nothing was too small for his attention. I clearly felt his interested reaction to each of my answers, each of my words, although he carefully tried to conceal it. He wanted to give our conversation the simple character of an ordinary, friendly chat, but he did not always succeed. When I began to praise one of the Moscow productions which had enjoyed public acclaim (I knew that Konstantin Sergeyevich had seen it), I suddenly saw such horror in his eyes that I had to stop without finishing the sentence. Only after the passing of many years did I understand how out of place my words had been.

Stanislavski attacked that theatre and its director, now angrily, now sarcastically, unmasking the defects in the basic principle of the production and finally, unexpectedly, he depicted the whole essence of the production by an extremely expressive demonstration. I involuntarily burst out laughing and that, it seemed to me, somehow soothed him.

A quiet, interesting conversation was reestablished. Konstantin Sergeyevich asked me a question, but I did not have time to answer before he was called to the telephone. Someone was calling him from the theatre. I heard quite clearly Stanislavski's conversation. It concerned a rather minor question about theatre life, but Stanislavski tried with all his passion, for the course of at least an hour, to get to the solution of the matter, not being satisfied with the fact that the caller kept agreeing with him. He tried to inculcate in the caller definite principles for solving such questions in the future.

Konstantin Sergeyevich was so excited by this conversation that, on returning to the table, for some time he looked at me with a malicious expression in his eyes, as if taking me for his telephone caller. When I timidly tried to answer the question which had been put to me one hour before, without listening to the end of my sentence, he sternly bellowed: "Nothing of the sort!" Then he came to his senses, gradually calmed down, and our conversation continued. Several times, fearing to take too much of his time, I tried to take leave, but he kept me. Finally the conversation came to a close. Seeing me to the front door, Konstantin Sergeyevich was very attentive and kind.

Stanislavski's attitude toward me during my visit, his sincere, penetrating remarks about art and his boundless dedication to the theatre made an impression on me which would be difficult to define now, but which has remained throughout my entire theatre life. The atmosphere, the whole character and condition of work, the interrelationship between the workers in the Theatre, which I later saw for the first time, strengthened this impression still more. I understood that I was standing on the threshold of something new, unknown and stirring, that something much greater had happened than just the moving from one theatre to another. Suddenly, as never before, I felt the importance of an event in my life.

My entrance into the creative life of the Moscow Art Theatre began with good luck. They were preparing to show Stanislavski a roughly rehearsed play, *The Embezzlers* by Katayev. It was several days before the demonstration performance and they were lacking a player for a small role. The director, Sudakov, offered the part to me. It was a comic role and the fact that I had to prepare it in two or three rehearsals did not disturb me. I was used to that. My performance in this part was successful to such an extent that Stanislavski decided to give me one of the important parts in this play—that of the cashier, Vanechka, which up to that time Khmelev, one of the principal actors of the theatre, had been rehearsing—and give my role to him. This was a great expression of Stanislavski's confidence in me. I was in seventh heaven. Everything is going so smoothly, so simply, I thought. My earlier fears of the difficulties I might encounter at the Moscow Art Theatre seemed no more than fantasies created by my imagination. Then in the autumn, after the summer recess, we began again to rehearse *The Embezzlers.*

The play, adapted from the novel, is dramatically quite loose and reminds one of a review: the bookkeeper, Philip Stepanovich, and the cashier, Vanechka, appropriate a sum of money and, in consequence, are drawn deeper and deeper into new crimes and adventures. Having spent the whole sum which they took, they are forced to return home and reveal their crime to the Criminal Investigation Department. In the course of the play the two "embezzlers" fall into very sharp dramatic and comic situations which give ample scope for acting.

According to the old stock-character terminology, the role of Vanechka is that of a simpleton, a role for which they had prepared me at the theatre school. I set to work with great excitement. But this was not the bit part which I had created independently and in which I first appeared so successfully. The role of Vanechka runs through the entire play and is joined with many other characters; it must harmonize with the ensemble and the general style of the whole production. The moment of difficulty came. No one could say that my playing at the Korsh Theatre was far from the style of the Moscow Art Theatre. On the contrary, my nearness to the style of the Moscow Art Theatre was the ground for my invitation to that theatre. All the same, when the need came to harmonize with the director and with the actors, some difficulties and roughness arose. At one point I even attempted to relinquish the role. But finally it seemed as if everything was going well; the play was prepared for showing to Stanislavski and the day of the demonstration arrived.

The demonstration took place not on the stage but in the

foyer of the theatre. This was a novelty for me; the "audience" was sitting almost in front of our noses, and what an audience! The actors were playing through scene after scene in unfinished sets. The acting had a somewhat sketchy character; it was more a demonstration of the design of the roles than a full presentation of them. For me this was unusual, but all the same, I somehow overcame most of the difficulties. Konstantin Sergeyevich approved of my performance and in general was satisfied with the result of the demonstration. I supposed that the opening of the play was but a question of time; in any case, there was no cause for worry, the chief difficulties had been overcome and the road to the Moscow Art Theatre footlights, to the Moscow Art Theatre audience was cleared. It remained only to polish my performance, but that would come from contact with the audience. How mistaken I was! From the moment Stanislavski joined the rehearsal, very serious and persistent work began; everything which had been done up to that point was no more than a rough preparation.

The work of Stanislavski on this play was exceptionally strenuous and energetic. The play, it seemed, was not turning out well. The actors were in difficulties. Even the old hands in the Moscow Art Theatre had trouble, and for a newcomer, to whom a great deal of attention was paid, each rehearsal turned into a sort of Calvary. But all that was made up for by what I was seeing for the first time, by the miracles being performed before my eyes. I left every rehearsal enriched, but discouraged. The new stage terms and the unaccustomed method of work confused me, constrained me, and I, an experienced actor, felt myself a bull in a china shop. What had happened to everything?

The first rehearsals with Stanislavski took place in the so-called C.O. hall, short for "Comic Opera." Rehearsals took place at the table with no mise en scéne. Konstantin Sergeyevich led the conversation, asked questions, gave explanations and tried to rehearse some scenes. By the way, rehearsal "at the table" was an innovation of the Moscow Art Theatre.

Although this was subjected to criticism by Stanislavski, he never disclaimed the value of such rehearsals in principle. In the old theatres, in the provinces as well as in the capital, only the first reading of a play by the actors took place at the table, where the text was checked, cuts were given and so forth. This was not even called a rehearsal but a "reading". After the reading, on the following day, the actors would go onstage and, with scripts in hand, rehearse the play, going through all of it from beginning to end. In the first rehearsals they used to set the mise en scéne, master it and then rehearse without scripts, each one trying to find the "correct tone" for his role; later, they held the general rehearsal in costumes and makeup, and only then did they "play" the play, each more or less on his own.

The directors of the Moscow Art Theatre, who were giving themselves more complicated tasks, naturally had to come to more perfect forms of rehearsals. One of these was the rehearsal at the table, where the future performers of the play, with the director at the head, subjected the separate units of the work to careful analysis, with much searching and even more experiments in embodiment. Stanislavski suggested that I play one of my scenes. Finding myself in a situation unusual for a rehearsal, deprived of the support of the mise en scéne, face to face with Stanislavski himself, I got somewhat confused, but my acting experience brought back my self-confidence, and I soon fell into that "true tone" which I had worked out in previous rehearsals. In general, I played the same as I had at the demonstration, but to my surprise I did not see any approval on the face of Konstantin Sergeyevich. After listening to the scene, he was silent for a while, then coughed and, smiling politely, said:

"Excuse me, Vasily Osipovich, but you have here a 'little tone'."

"What?"

"You want to play the part and have worked out a 'little tone' for it."

I didn't understand a thing. Well, yes, but how could it be otherwise? Naturally, I had a tone. What was wrong with that? I had searched long and agonizingly for that "little tone." After all, hadn't he approved of me in the demonstration? What had happened, then? I confessed that I understood nothing of what he was saying. Konstantin Sergeyevich then explained to me that the most valuable thing in creative work is the ability, first of all, to find the living person, to find oneself, in each part.

"You have bound yourself to something thought out in advance and this hinders you from perceiving organically what is going on around you. You are playing a stereotype, not a living person."

"Yes, but how . . ."

"Tell me, what do you have in your office?"

"I don't understand."

"You are a cashier, aren't you? What do you have in your office?"

"Money . . ."

"Well, yes, money. But what else? Tell me in more detail. You say 'money.' Good, how much? What kind? How is it folded? Where is it kept? What kind of table do you have in your office? What kind of chair, how many electric lights? Well, tell me about all your surroundings in more detail."

I was silent a long time. He waited patiently for my answer. Finally I admitted that I could not answer even one of his questions, and I did not understand very well why I should know all that. Ignoring my last remark, he suggested that I think for a little while and answer at least one of his questions. I was silent.

"You see, you don't know the most vital things about your character—about his daily affairs, what life means to him, what concerns him.

"Here is the cashier Vanechka. A kind, modest young man. He is at home in his cashier's office, it is his holy of holies. It is the best thing that he has in his life. Everything there is the object of his concern: both the cleanliness of the premises and the arrangement of all the objects he uses daily, beginning with the large steel safe and ending with his favorite red and blue pencil, which he considers his best friend and calls 'Konstantin Sidorovich.' He keeps the electric lamp so clean, it is the brightest source of light in the whole accounting department. This is Vanechka's pride. The locks of the fireproof safe, lubricated with fat, lock and unlock easily. Their pleasant clicking delights Vanechka; he listens to them as to beautiful music. On the shelf of the safe, packages of bills are arranged in model order. Here are hundreds, thousands, tens, hundreds of thousands. Vanechka can always tell exactly how much there is at any given moment. The very process of giving out money and the payroll excites him. These are religious rites for Vanechka. He lives through tragedy with the employees, when, because of the absence of sufficient money, he cannot pay them. Vanechka never makes errors in counting; his accuracy is legendary. In spite of his youth and modesty, he is a sort of celebrity in the bookkeeping world, and he does not value anything so much as this reputation.

"The head bookkeeper, Philip Stepanovich, loves him. Vanechka, for his part, worships Philip Stepanovich as an ordinary soldier might worship a great captain. The smallest infringement of this world of Vanechka's was always an event for him, causing emotional shocks. What if (God preserve us!) his Konstantin Sidorovich should be lost? Or the light bulb be found covered with fly specks? Or if someone signed the payroll in the wrong column? All these make up those official disasters of which Vanechka can talk endlessly in his free time. It is terrible to think what would happen if some sort of monetary error should be found, if a few bills should be missing from the pack. Such events have not yet happened in his life; he can only visualize them as in a bad dream.

"Now imagine the feelings of Vanechka when, after a series of diabolic coincidences, he wakes from a drunken stupor to find himself in a sleeping compartment on a train to

Leningrad with ten thousand embezzled rubles, the chief bookkeeper in a drunken sleep and a woman of easy virtue in the upper berth.

"What deviltry, what a monstrous destruction of Vanechka's marvelous world, what a tragedy in his life!

"But you didn't create that world, you didn't feel it inwardly, you didn't try to embody it on the stage. It's not important that the author doesn't show it. In the cashier's office during the action, when the window is closed and nobody sees you, or even before the start of the rehearsal, in this, your own little cubicle, did you try by yourself to really live by these small bits of your role: to dust, to clean the lamp bulb, to put the money in piles, to sharpen the pencil, etc.?

"No. In that time, at best, you tested your intonation, you thought how you would deliver your first lines, you planned what you would do when you would open the window of your cashier's booth and the part of your role seen by the audience would begin. You didn't create the roots through which your role will be nourished."

I understood that there was deep truth in this, but I didn't understand at all how it could be worked out practically. How, then, to rehearse further? I tried to argue; I demonstrated the possibility of another method of work, spoke of the results achieved by me earlier, but all my arguments were easily torn down, one after the other, by the logic of Stanislavski.

"But I played parts of it very well, didn't I?"

"It's very possible, but don't you want to play better?"

"Certainly."

"I am showing you the way to do that. Besides that, I want to spare you unnecessary, painful wanderings on wrong paths during your work on a role."

I didn't give up; for a long time I persisted. Konstantin Sergeyevich, sighing deeply, said:

"What a debater we have invited to our theatre!"

So, the rehearsal didn't go beyond my first scene. Such an

unproductive waste of time seemed to me, at that time, astonishing; at the Korsh Theatre we would have been able to get through the whole play. But the ideas put into my head by Stanislavski took possession of me with surprising strength and fermented in me right up to the following rehearsal. It was held without Stanislavski, but in an improvised setting and with props. I diffidently tried to perform everything which he had recommended, but I was somehow so unaccustomed to it that I blushed each time someone watched what I was doing.

No, this was all some sort of deviltry! How simple everything had been before; at the Korsh you had the mise en scène, a partner, cues—you could play. But here . . . Still, I had to try it once more. Having looked around, I again started to dust, to sharpen the pencil, to put things in order. No, something was wrong. I was doing all this before the rehearsal, which had not yet begun although the sets and props were already in place.

Suppose I try once more, seriously, completely realistically. Here in front of me stands my little table. I will put it in really ideal order. Here is some dust, here a spot, I must try to remove both. I try to do this with all honesty. I achieve something. So, further, the table is shaky—I have to make it stand firm. I am not successful; I try to find something to put under the leg. I find a sliver of wood, I shove it under the leg. The table does not swing any more, it is perfectly stable. . . . Now I have to put all the objects in perfect order.

I did not notice how completely fascinated I had become with all these things. It was very pleasant to be occupied with this stage business. Here lies my little knife and my pencil—suppose I try to sharpen it perfectly. I start this work with all my attention and with pleasure, but . . . what is it? Something moved, people began to appear. . . . Oh! the rehearsal is commencing. My cue has come, I open the cash window and begin my scene.

From one day to the next the rehearsals of *The Embezzlers* proceeded, at times under the direction of Stanislavski, at other times without him. Each rehearsal with Stanislavski, especially of my scenes, struck me with ever newer and more unexpected methods of work. Everything was interesting, fascinating, but, it seemed to me, with little relationship to our eventual performance.

Well, good, I may achieve some results along the line of which he speaks, but this is mostly that which will not be shown to the audience. And the scene itself which I will have to play, what will happen to it? Stanislavski, strange as it may seem, was interested least of all in the text which would be spoken before the audience. I didn't have time to open my mouth before he stopped me, paying attention to some "trifles" which seemingly had no relation to the action.

"Well, let me say at least one sentence! Maybe something will come out of it."

"Nothing will come out if you are not prepared."

"But, I worked . . ."

"Not on the right thing. All your preparation has not brought you to this scene which you have to play. Consequently, there is no use filling your ears with false intonations which will be difficult to get rid of later. Don't think of the lines, the intonations—they will come of themselves. Think, rather, of your behavior. You, only you and not anyone else, have to distribute several thousand rubles to payroll clerks gathered outside the cashier's window. You are responsible for every kopek. How will you act? Keep in mind that all payroll clerks are cheats. You must be careful. How will you accomplish this? How will you start? What have you prepared? What kind of documents do you need? Do you have enough money? Opening the window, you estimate, according to the number of people, approximately what sum is needed to satisfy them. Perhaps you can limit the distribution to fifty percent? Create for yourself in this job a sequence of individual concerns and act accordingly. Believe me, this is most interesting; the audience will follow this; it is by this most of all that you will convince them of the reality of what is going on. Can you see how much there is here besides words? Words and intonations are the result of your thoughts, your actions, but you, I see, omit everything which in life cannot ever be omitted—you opened the cash window and waited for your cue while preparing your intonations. But from whence can they come, how can they be living, organic, when you break the simplest laws of human behavior?"

And then we would begin to busy ourselves with the bookkeeper's tasks: counting money, checking the documents, the columns, etc. But again the thought of losing time disturbs me: We must rehearse the *play!* I have a big part. It is true, sometimes this play accounting carries me away. Sometimes I succeed in believing in the seriousness of what is going on, and at such moments, if I can utter one or another line from my role, it sounds very warm and truthful and calls forth a good reaction from those present. But all that seemed to me something that appeared accidentally and could as easily vanish forever. So it was: as soon as I had the wish to fix something, to repeat it exactly, nothing would come out. In this work I did not feel the assurance to which I was accustomed when previously working on a role. At that time there had been, first, the reading of the play, followed by the reading by roles, the establishment of the mise en scènes, the search for the general "tone" of the role, the invention of particular intonations and "tricks"; in short, the gradual piling up of all those elements which were considered dear to the audience. The real meaning of Stanislavski's method of work was not clear to me at that time. Here, during very intensive, very active rehearsal work, nobody gives any thought to the final result, that is, to the final performance; here the future audience is somehow ignored and, however strange it may seem, much more attention is given to things which the audience will never see.

I do not say that my bewilderment about all I saw at the Moscow Art Theatre gave rise to disillusionment with it. On the contrary, everything fascinated me very much, awakened my mind and my imagination and aroused the desire to understand. It was as if I were living anew the first year of my theatrical training when I absorbed my first ideas about the technique of our wonderful art with such awe. But, all the same, the new method of work seemed to me somewhat revolutionary.

Only after many years did the amazing harmony of the whole system of Stanislavski, the director, teacher and leader of the Theatre, become clear to me; only then did I see that it was a system of work which united in rehearsal all those facets of his activity. I eventually understood the different stages in Konstantin Sergeyevich's work in the development of a play and realized that no one else felt so early as he the form of the future play or took such care that its clarity be made apparent to the audience. To accomplish this, he had special means which were not very clear to me at that time.

During its development, the work on *The Embezzlers* took on new forms all the time. The rehearsals of some scenes aready had been transferred to the stage. There, gradually clearer mise en scènes took shape but, to my amazement, the director did not insist that the actors adhere to them; furthermore, moments of improvisation were frequent.

On the stage was the apartment of the old bookkeeper. His family, which consisted of his wife and two children, was in some anxiety. It was already long past the dinner hour and the master still was not home. At the moment of highest tension a sharp bell was heard. The wife ran to open the door and before her stood her husband, the bookkeeper, and the cashier Vanechka, completely drunk, but in a very festive mood. The bookkeeper, when they had dropped in at an ale house earlier, had concocted a plan to marry his daughter to the cashier. With this in mind they have come home, bringing with them wine and food. But the bookkeeper's wife, a very temperamental Polish woman, meets them with such a stream of swearing as Vanechka probably has never heard before, and he becomes frightened. The bookkeeper, wishing to stop the row which threatens to grow into violence, with difficulty pushes his wife into the other room to talk to her. Vanechka remains alone, very frightened and depressed. After standing for a while, he begins to listen to what is going on between the bookkeeper and his wife in their room, from which he can hear excited voices, but he cannot make out a word. Vanechka approaches the door, bends down and looks through the keyhole. Seeing that the enraged woman is coming toward him, he jumps away from the door.

"Well, sir, what would you do?" asked Stanislavski.

"I beg your pardon . . . ?"

"You are left alone in the room . . . under all these circumstances. Take into consideration what has happened to you and what you must do. This is your scene."

"But there is nothing here. He is simply standing; then he goes to the door, eavesdrops, peeps through the keyhole and jumps away. There is nothing more."

"That is not enough for you? Well, all right. Go and simply look through the keyhole, listen at the door. . . . Stop! Are you listening now? Are you?"

"Yes, I am."

"No. You are trying to *act* something. You must *listen*. You cannot hear anything, can you? Why do you want to listen at the door?"

"Out of curiosity."

"I don't believe it. Well, never mind, simply put your ear to the door. What would you do if you absolutely had to make out what is going on in that room? You want to act something all the time. Didn't you ever have to eavesdrop? Try to remember how you did it. No? Well, let's say you didn't. Go on, go and look through the keyhole. Suppose someone suddenly pushed a knitting needle through the keyhole. How would you jump away from the door . . . ? That's awful! I don't believe anything. Not a single movement. Do it again. . . . I still don't believe you. What is hindering you? Well, try once more. . . . Why are you so tense?"

We repeated the same thing again and again, scores of times. Finally, it looked as if we had achieved something.

"Very good, but with a little plus."

"What?"

"With a little plus."

"I do not understand what that means."

"It's done correctly, but you added a little to the correctness, a hardly noticeable little plus. Obviously, you did it to make the audience laugh."

"And isn't that necessary? It *is* a funny scene, isn't it?"

"It will be still funnier if you do only as much as is necessary. That is the most expressive way. Every addition, every little plus, produces only false, so-called 'theatricality.' To find the *true measure* is the most difficult thing in our art. Well, go and try again."

Again helpless repetitions of the same thing until finally, when angered to a degree and obviously not wishing to play any more, I simply bent to the keyhole and jumped away; a burst of laughter sounded in the room. I didn't understand a thing; either it was really good or they were laughing at me.

"That was absolutely correct. Look always for just that. Do you understand? Well, let's go on."

I must confess I still understood little, but I remembered the phrase "little plus."

The cashier, Vanechka, was a nice, modest youth. He was transformed into an embezzler quite by chance, through the concurrence of circumstances of fate. His daily interests, the activities of his job already have been described, but there is something else which may be the dearest thing to him—the village of Berezovka, where he had spent his childhood in a ramshackle cottage where his old mother still lives.

So the two embezzlers, the old bookkeeper and the cashier, tossing to right and left hundreds and thousands of rubles, journey from town to town experiencing various circumstances of life until by chance, or perhaps not by chance, they reach a little town not far from Vanechka's village. Meeting some peasants in an inn disturbs and excites the drunken Vanechka, who tells them that he is from this very region. He explains where the village of Berezovka is and where the cottage is in which his little mother . . .

This monologue of Vanechka demands great emotion from the actor. Thousands of thoughts and feelings arise in the unhappy young man when he remembers what was for him so dear and now seems lost forever. For me this was the place in the role for which all the rest existed.

In former times, I would have begun work on the role with this monologue. But now everything is different. We just cannot get to this scene; we are continually occupied with all kinds of trifles. *When* will I get to it? I will show them then what genuine feeling, what real temperament is. I do not think that they will reproach me then with "little pluses."

I spent many nights at home on this monologue trying to say it in every possible way, trying my utmost to kindle my feelings. Sometimes I succeeded and tears ran down my cheeks at the closing sentence, "Here lives . . . my little mother."

Finally the day of rehearsal with Stanislavski arrived. Having begun my monologue, I was afraid, above everything else, that he would interrupt me and so dampen my ardor. But contrary to all my expectations, Konstantin Sergeyevich did not do that and listened to the monologue to the end. However, the expected effect did not come; only pitiful pangs and a sentimental quavering voice. I was embarrassed and spoke first:

"Nothing will come."

"And what did you expect?"

"At home this monologue turned out very well."

"What do you mean exactly?"

"There was much feeling . . . I even cried."

"Exactly! You were afraid of losing those feelings. A completely wrong task. That is exactly what spoiled it. Does Vanechka think of that while speaking to the peasants? No.

And you must not think of it either. Why should you cry? Let the audience cry."

"But it seems to me that it would be more touching."

"Nothing of the sort! That is cheap sentimentality. Untalented beggars act in that way, and it always brings the opposite result. They only irritate people. What does Vanechka do here? What does he want from the peasants? Only one thing: that they will tell him the way to where his mother lives. The way is very complicated; the peasants are quite stupid. Do you understand how active such a task can be? Is this a time for tears? Do you clearly imagine all the roads, the paths and landmarks to the village of Berezovka—the way to your mother's cottage? I think you don't, judging by the way you played just now. And this is most important. Imagine the difficult, tangled topography of the country and try to picture it clearly, all the time watching each of the peasants to see whether he understands you correctly. Get out of your head all concern for your own emotional experiences and feelings."

Suddenly a recollection flashed through my mind. I continued to rehearse. The monologue finally was successful, and Konstantin Sergeyevich was satisfied. When the rehearsal ended and I went home, I thought again about the memory that had flashed across my mind.

Several years before entering the Moscow Art Theatre I had rehearsed a comedy at the Korsh Theatre. The hero of the play in which I acted, a failure who found himself overcome with difficulties, was forced for the sake of money to undertake a daredevil act in a film; he had to jump from a high rock into the sea at great risk to his life. Just before the jump he turns directly to the audience for sympathy and delivers an extensive monologue full of dramatic tension in which he states his last wish. He begins by telling about the unhappy fate which cased him to risk his life. He does not believe in a happy outcome of the jump, and therefore takes leave of all those present. In the final words of the monologue he asks the audience to remember him when, after his death, they go to the cinema with their girl friends and see him disappearing into the chasm of nonexistence; let them remember . . . and so on and so on.

The monologue is quite touching, it is written very warmly, dramatically, but with some humor, as is fitting in a comedy with a happy ending. I liked this monologue very much. I decided that the happy ending of the play should not be predetermined, but that this scene should be played with a seriousness corresponding to the event. The monologue must move the audience to the utmost, in order that the happy ending should bring them as much joy as possible.

Working on this monologue, I tried to find the key to the fullest expression of my feelings. Sometimes I succeeded, sometimes I didn't. At one rehearsal I was completely successful. My friends applauded and congratulated me. I was very happy. On the whole, the role was successful; it had needed only this last touch. It was now there and everying was in order. At the following rehearsal, approaching the monologue, I anticipated the pleasure of having still more success. But it didn't happen; I was overcome with disappointment. With the first sentence of the monologue I felt something false and no matter how I tried to correct myself, to find what had been so good at the rehearsal the day before, nothing worked; on the contrary, the more I tried, the worse it became. There was not one live intonation, not one flash of live feeling; everything was dead, empty, false. In complete bewilderment I was ready to hide in shame. Well, no matter, tomorrow I would try again to be better, more attentive. Tonight at home I would work some more and everything would be all right. Failure is natural.

However, in the succeeding rehearsals, things got worse and worse. In spite of all my efforts, the feeling which once had arisen no longer returned. One thing remained—the actor's usual consolation—a conviction that the feeling would arise at the performance before the audience.

The dress rehearsal was a complete failure. Finally, after a sleepless night and an agonizing day, I went to the performance. From my first scene everything went well; success grew from scene to scene. Shortly before the monologue there was loud applause. I felt in myself a great buildup of deeping feeling and creative joy. If I could only guard this and not lose it before the monologue! I tried not to be distracted by anything; I avoided my comrades, stayed by myself. Finally, here it was, the fatal moment. Going out upon the stage, I said the first sentence; someone in the audience coughed, annoyingly, at the end of it. That angered me, but I restrained myself. I must not lose my feelings! I continued to deliver the monologue, but for some reason I said the words very quietly, as if I were afraid of spilling something which was inside me. But to my horror, I felt that there was nothing inside any more. The audience began to cough more and more, and I began to be angry with them and with myself. Finally I decided to exaggerate a little; it became even worse—false, trivial, theatrical. The audience by this time had lost all interest in my character, and I finished the monologue indistinctly, garbling the words. I left the stage in embarrassment to perform my "fatal" leap with the audience completely indifferent to my fate.

The role, three-quarters of which had been well played, could be considered a complete failure, since the chief moment was not successful. Further performances were repetitions of the opening night. I did not know what to do to bring back the once-experienced feelings, none of which came to me again. They say that art is difficult, that one must work. I understood all that. I was ready to work in order to conquer that accursed monologue, but how? What should I do? The harder I tried, the worse everything turned out. I was overcome with the feeling, well-known to every actor, of shame for my lack of talent. Protecting myself from this disgusting feeling, in one of the performances, I assumed a tone of indifference and cynicism toward the play and toward my part, especially when things were approaching the fatal moment. Just before the monologue, I chattered with my comrades backstage, recounted anecdotes, laughed, winked at my partner. With complete indifference I went onstage, looked calmly at the nearest member of the audience, and jokingly threw the first line at him point-blank. He pricked up his ears and became interested. Ah, you are interested—then here is some more for you. . . . I see that those sitting next to him are listening attentively. Encouraged by this, I began to develop my idea further. The audience became quiet. I felt that the whole theatre was becoming interested. I began to be anxious. Could they hear me in the gallery? Do they catch my thoughts? I addressed them also. I felt that they understood me very well and sympathized with me. I continued my "conversation" with more and more enthusiasm and animation and, after finishing my monologue with persistent demands that after my death those seated in the hall should come to see the picture and remember me in the moment of deadly flight, I left the stage to great applause.

See what happens? Everything comes in reverse. It is not at all necessary to concentrate on the role; on the contrary, one must be diverted from it in every possible way. It is very simple and easy. I had discovered a new law! This was no actor's trickery; everything happened convincingly and realistically. At what doors had I not knocked, and all for nothing, and here, suddenly, such an unexpected success. . . .

But at the following performance my hopes collapsed, and my "discovery" proved false. I came to hate the part. Fortunately for me, the play closed. However, for a long time I did not recover from the shock I had received. And now, many years later, rehearsing the monologue of Vanechka with Stanislavski, I remember my former struggles and am amazed at the simple means this remarkable master uses to liberate the actor's creative possibilities, to create room for him to bring to light his live, true feelings. Now I understand that *maximum concentration* and *genuine attention* are the indispensable conditions for penetration into a stage character. Before everything else one must find the right direction for this concentration. My failure in that ill-fated play was the consequence of wandering along incorrect paths. By chance I came upon a true path which brought me success. But the rejection of a wrong path does not necessarily mean that one will find the unique path of active, genuine, organic action. Stanislavski led me to this path in rehearsals of the Vanechka scenes, and I found it by chance in the scene just described when, having made contact with one person seated in the audience and having received from him an answering response, I gradually drew the whole audience into the orbit of my attention. Does not the same task stand before Vanechka when he speaks to the peasants about his mother? But in the former play I had to make direct contact, not with the people who were on the stage, which is usual for the dramatic actor, but with those sitting in the audience, which almost never happens in our practice. That was exactly, it seemed to me, the chief cause of my difficulty.

The rehearsals with Stanislavski gave impetus to my thoughts in this direction. It is natural that at that time they could not have even the approximate clarity with which I narrate this incident today. *The importance of the tranference of the actor's attention from the search for feelings inside himself to the fulfillment of the stage task which actively influences his partners* is one of Stanislavski's greatest discoveries; this discovery resolved many problems of our technique and freed countless actors from agonizing worry.

Does this mean that Stanislavski denied the emotional side of our creativity completely? Not at all. He often spoke of it, but he considered that stage mastery only exists as a high art when the artist puts into it genuine passion and living temperament.

Many years after the rehearsal I have described, I talked with Stanislavski about "creative feeling," the concentration of the actor onstage and other matters which had a close relationship to the rehearsal of *The Embezzlers* and to what had happened when I delivered my final monologue at the Korsh

Theatre. I brought up the fact that concentration and a serious attitude toward a role do not always give the best results. There is a conviction among many actors that a portion of lightness, indifference or cynicism toward their work frequently brings them much greater success. Every actor knows that if, for some reason, he wants to play especially well, he will inevitably play poorly. This is often the case when someone "special" is watching the performance. The actor braces himself, but in most cases the result is complete failure.

I hinted to Konstantin Sergeyevich that I was rather of the same opinion because I had had the chance more than once to observe this in my own practice, especially when I performed as a reciter. I succeeded in this art very seldom, and this was invariably on those evenings when I was in a hurry to go somewhere after the reading. In such cases only one thought possessed me: To read through quickly and go.

"And why do you think that you read well then?"

"From my own feelings and . . ."

"And . . ."

"And from my success with the public."

"Both may have been delusions."

"Well, at the end the organizers and others who heard my reading said that . . ."

"Hm, hm, such potboilers. When you played badly, it was not the result of attentiveness and concentration or of a serious approach; it was simply that you concentrated on something which was not called for. When you discarded the false concentration which hindered you, it turned out better. But if you can direct your genuine attention and concentration on fulfilling the concrete task in a scene, it will be very good."

I did not get an understanding of rhythm either in theatre school or from any of the directors with whom I had been associated in my earlier work. Although I had often heard this word from theatre workers in the years before my entrance

into the Moscow Art Theatre, I had never received a clear
explanation of it. Up to that time this most important question, in its application to our stage art, remained obscure.

I am ashamed to confess this now. "Rhythm," "tempo,"
"tempo-rhythm," "rhythm-tempo," these words are now frequently on the lips of directors, actors and critics. But try to get
an exact explanation of the meaning of these words from any
one of them and he will not be able to satisfy your curiosity. He
will answer your question in general terms which cannot have
any practical application. In olden times there existed in theatre terminology the universal word "tone." There was a tone
for the part and a general tone for the play, and the actor could
find or miss the tone. The performance might be running in a
lowered tone, and the actor coming onstage could be asked in
the middle of the action to "raise the tone." No one knew
exactly how this could be done; the actor would usually just
start talking louder than the others. This, of course, turned out
to be futile; the actor did not find the tone, he quickly lost his
vitality, and the performance continued running in the same
lowered tone until something happened, not dependent on the
will of the participants, which saved the situation and the tone
of the performance would rise to the desired pitch. Later, each
actor would take the credit for this and it became the subject of
many disputes. These arguments were never solved because no
one, in reality, understood what had happened or knew exactly
what the tone of the performance really was, about which
everybody was so concerned. Only after persistent searching
was Stanislavski able to define his idea of "rhythm" and put into
practice his knowledge in this field. I saw long, drawn-out
rehearsals transformed miraculously into full-blooded conflicts
of great intensity. This was the consequence of Stanislavski's
mastery, the result of his ability to put his very definite ideas of
stage rhythm into practice.

So, for example, we rehearsed a small scene from *The
Embezzlers*. The senior bookkeeper, traveling by train with his
cashier, Vanechka, has fallen in with some card sharks and,

joining their game, risks losing everything that remains of the embezzled money. This frightens the poor cashier terribly. At a station stop, the bookkeeper, interrupting the game, springs out of the coach into the station buffet for a glass of vodka. The station stop is very short. Vanechka, jumping out of the train after his partner, hopes to persuade him not to return to the train or, at least, to turn his attention to something so that he will not notice when the train leaves. But, consumed with excitement, the bookkeeper is not so easily deceived. He is possessed by the desire to win back his losses as quickly as possible and it is very difficult to keep him in the buffet when the station bell rings, giving notice of the imminent departure of the train. All the more so since Vaneckha has very little to say—the author has given him nothing with the exception of one exclamation: "Philip Stepanovich! Philip Stepanovich!"

The scene did not go well, and I felt that the blame for this lay with me, but I put it on the author: really now, what can be done with only one phrase at your disposal? It was easy for Tarkhanov, who had plenty of words, to play something, but I had just two words: "Philip Stepanovich! Philip Stepanovich!" And that was all.

Imagine my amazement when Konstantine Sergeyevich said:

"Vasily Osipovich, take into consideration that this is your scene; here you have the chief role, not Tarkhanov."

"Yes, but here I have nothing to say except 'Philip Stepanovich!' "

"It doesn't matter. You have a very active task: to hold back the bookkeeper by any means and keep him from the train. How you do this will show your mastery."

"Yes, but I have no words, it is very hard."

"It is not a question of words. Try at the same time to watch both Tarkhanov and the train standing on the track on the point of leaving. This is your only salvation. Well, try."

It is easy to say "try"! But how? I stood in confusion.

"Well, where is Tarkhanov, and where is the train? Try to

define all this exactly for yourself. Watch Tarkhanov. What is he doing? And what about the train? Do you feel the rhythm of the scene?"

Here it was, the word "rhythm!" I still did not have the slightest notion what it meant.

Stanislavski persisted: "You are not standing in the correct rhythm!"

To stand in rhythm! How—to stand in a rhythm! To walk, to dance, to sing in rhythm—this I could understand, but to *stand!*

"Really, would you stand in such a way if such serious consequences threatened you as the departure of Tarkhanov on the train?"

"Pardon me, Konstantin Sergeyevich, but I have no idea whatsoever what rhythm is."

"That is not important. Around that corner is a mouse. Take a stick and lie in wait for it; kill it as soon as it jumps out.... No, that way you will let it escape. Watch more attentively—*more attentively.* As soon as I clap my hands, beat it with the stick.... Ah, see how late you are! Once more. Concentrate more. Try to make the stroke of the stick almost simultaneous with the clap. Well then, do you see that now you are standing in a completely different rhythm than before? Do you feel the difference? To stand and watch for a mouse—that is one rhythm; to watch a tiger that is creeping up on you is quite another one. Watch Tarkhanov attentively, take into account his every movement. Just now he forgot about the train, he was carried away by the food. This is fortunate for you—you can calm down for a moment and look at what the train is doing. You can even run out onto the platform for a moment; but come back immediately. Then all your attention must again be on the bookkeeper, Tarkhanov. Try to guess his intentions, to understand his thoughts. Now he remembers the train, fumbles in his pockets to pay for the vodka. Organize yourself to distract him, to hold him in the buffet at whatever cost. Your readiness to complete the action will force you both to move and stand in different rhythms from what you do now. Well, try it."

This element in our technique, rhythm, interested me greatly. I continued to rehearse with enthusiasm, tried to grasp the essence of this matter, but it didn't work. I didn't succeed in anything in which Stanislavski had prompted me. At times a superficial sense of urgency and bustle would arise but without any real communication with my partner.

Stanislavski admirably demonstrated his own skill in using different rhythms. He would take the simplest episode from everyday life—for example, buying a newspaper at a stand in the station—and play it in completely different rhythms. He would buy a paper when there is a whole hour before the departure of the train and he doesn't know how to kill the time, or when the first or second bell has rung, or when the train has already started. The actions are all the same but in completely different rhythms, and Konstantin Sergeyevich was able to carry out these exercises in any order: by increasing the rhythm, by diminishing the rhythm, by sudden change. I saw the mastery, I saw the technique, the tangible technique of our art. He had mastered all this thanks to persistent work on himself.

This excited me more than anything I had seen in the previous rehearsals with Stanislavski. I myself could not do anything yet, but I understood that this was something very important in our work, and I felt that in time it would be possible to master it fully; here I saw something similiar to technical musical exercises or etudes.

As a former musician, I knew that one and the same etude may be played in different rhythms, in different styles as one tries to achieve different objectives. I knew well the feeling of satisfaction that comes when one has overcome the stiffness of the fingers and they acquire confidence, flexibility, dexterity. A musician never doubts that such exercises, conscientiously and persistently practiced over a period of time, will advance the development of his technique. After the demonstration Stanislavski gave with the newspaper, I saw an affinity between our technique and that of the other arts.

"Well then, all this is very simple; just try to start living in a different rhythm. Now, rhythm may be found even in the simplest actions. Sit down quickly, now get up, again sit down, change quickly ten or twenty times a second without thinking about it. How would you direct it if you were the director of this scene? No, this is 'andante,' and here it should be 'presto.' Understand? Will you succeed or not in keeping Tarkhanov in the buffet? This is a matter of life or death for you. If in reality it were so, would you really think so long? How would you act?"

Somehow we didn't notice how we had been carried away by this original game. Tarkhanov strove to leave the room; I had to restrain him, but without touching him—that was the indispensable condition. This game soon took on the character of a serious competition, each of us trying to excel in the struggle. Stanislavski at once evaluated the situation but kept quiet. This was what he had wanted. The game went on with more and more excitement. Suddenly a bell rang, signaling the departure of the train. We slackened our pace.

"Why did you stop?"

"That's the end, the train is leaving. Further struggle has no meaning."

"Nothing of the kind, here it starts in full measure! That was only the second bell, there will still be a third, and later a whistle. Only after the whistle may you calm down; by then the outcome of the struggle will be decided. Meanwhile, the intensification goes on; the rhythm sharpens more and more. Continue."

We renewed our struggle and Konstantin Sergeyevich ordered that the third bell and the whistle should be given only at his signal. He held us in the most strenuous struggle for perhaps another twenty minutes, yet we didn't feel our inventiveness drying up. On the contrary, fired by enthusiasm, we developed our theme all the more deeply, more intensively, with more variety, and when finally the engine whistle blew, giving notice of the departure of the train and of the end of the struggle between the bookkeeper and the cashier, I was even a little sorry to stop our fascinating game. It had been so pleasant to feel in myself this full pulsation! Inventing ways of communicating with my partner made me happy. I was struck that such a scene could be created out of nothing. Wasn't there written in my notebook only the repetition of one and the same phrase: "Philip Stepanovich! Philip Stepanovich!" Any actor in my place would have said, as I did, "There is nothing to act here." And yet, just see what had happened!

This scene had only secondary importance in the play and therefore later it was greatly shortened. This epidsode could not be played in the way I described it in rehearsal; but the work we had done had a very beneficial influence on us. It was in rehearsals of this scene that I got my first, vague understanding of stage rhythm, which later on, developing and getting more and more accurate, became often a really miraculous means of solving stage problems.

The rehearsals of *The Embezzlers* continued, and in each of them something new was revealed to me. Already in the rehearsals, the outlines of the future performance began to be evident. Soon the run-through would begin. The work of Stanislavski then took on an altogether different character. But, even then, it sometimes happened that he would stop for a long time merely on the entrance of an actor. This occurred when we were rehearsing the scene in the compartment of the train where the bookkeeper and the cashier mistook the agent of a lithograph firm for a representative of the Criminal Investigation Bureau. Stanislavski unexpectedly turned his attention to the entrance of the agent and with unusual persistence tried to achieve certain objectives which were not clear to us. He found fault with every trifle, every movement. This painstaking work stretched out for two or three hours, at least. We all began to lose patience, especially the actor playing the

agent. Each of us wondered what would happen next, when
we rehearsed the actual scene. But Konstantin Sergeyevich, at
last having got the result he wanted from the actor who was
playing the agent (and his entrance into the compartment
turned out to be, indeed, marvelous), looked as if he had lost
interest in what was coming next. We understood at last what
he had wanted to achieve: he wanted the lithograph agent to
enter the compartment the way only an investigator tracing a
criminal would. The effect was striking, and Tarkhanov and I,
involuntarily, became really afraid. We played the scene with
great sincerity.

"At the most tense moment, try to light a cigarette. Your
lips tremble and the flame of the match misses the cigarette."

Tarkhanov did this with astonishing mastery. Those present burst into laughter.

After this Konstantin Sergeyevich looked at all the proper-
ties carefully. There were children's toys, which the bookkeeper had won somewhere. The toys were made rather
crudely. After looking at them, Stanislavski turned to Tarkhanov and said:

"We must use better toys; these do not harmonize with
your fine acting."

Then he went on to the next scene.

I must say again, such stopping at separate scenes had by
now become the exception rather than the rule. Greater problems occupied his attention now—problems of putting together all that which had been worked out in the rehearsals—
the creation of the play itself.

Finally the play opened. There were many good things in
it. Tarkhanov and Batalov played very well and there were
some interesting moments in the direction. But the weak dramatic material and the lack of an engrossing idea in the play
lowered the quality of the production. Konstantin Sergeyevich, with all his mastery, was unable to pull anything out
of this formless and shallow dramatic work. All the audience
saw was a series of expertly produced and brilliantly played

episodes. This could not satisfy such a master as Stanislavski. The work on the play caused him much anxiety and suffering. In a letter which Konstantin Sergeyevich sent me from Nice on the occasion of my twenty-fifth anniversary in the theatre, he wrote: "I recall the difficult but joyful work on *Dead Souls* and the difficult but joyless work on *The Embezzlers.*" Whether I played the role of Vanechka well or not was never clear to me. This was my first part at the Moscow Art Theatre and the question of success or failure was extremely important for me. Reviews about my playing were diverse: complimentary, neutral and negative. "Here is an actor who was brilliant but as soon as they started to teach him, his talent withered!"

The play did not last long in the repertory, but during its run I got into the role little by little and I started to have moments of success which the audience sometimes even applauded. This, of course, pleased me. It did not happen at the first performance, however. "Finally," I thought, "the fruits of Stanislavski's work! What a pity he cannot see the performance. No matter, someday he will see it."

In the spring, with Stanislavski at its head, the Moscow Art Theatre went on a guest tour to Leningrad. *The Embezzlers* was in the repertory. For me Leningrad had special significance. It was, first of all, my birthplace. My fondest memories were connected with it: the theatrical school, the Alexandrinsky and Suvorinsky theatres where my creative activity had begun.

In Leningrad I had many acquaintances and friends, many of whom were present at the rehearsal of *The Embezzlers,* some as extras in the crowd scenes, others as spectators who had come to observe the directing of Stanislavski. The atmosphere during the rehearsal was extremely thrilling for me. Everyone knows how painstakingly Konstantin Sergeyevich worked in the rehearsals of a revival of a play, especially when it concerned a guest appearance of the Moscow Art Theatre. But I was not worried; my role was polished and I was eager to show the brilliance of my acting both to Stanislavski and to those present at the Leningrad rehearsal, my acquaintances and friends.

The rehearsal began with the scene in the tavern, because that was a difficult crowd scene; the first part of the scene goes on without me. I run in later. Until my entrance everything went smoothly. But then my turn came; I waited for my cue impatiently and finally came running on stage. I liked very much the way I came running, that day especially. Suddenly:

"Stop!"

The rehearsal stopped, everyone stood stock still. I did not understand the reason for the interruption. In any case, I did not think it was because of me; that day I was at my best.

"What a horror! What are you doing? Who taught you this?" Then, after whispering to the assistants, "I am speaking to you, Vasily Osipovich!"

I was astonished.

"What is the matter?"

"My good fellow, in Kharkov they play that way. That's horrible!"

I looked askance at my Leningrad friends, who were gazing at me with curiosity and pity from the orchestra.

"Be so good as to do it again."

Again I came running and again, "Stop!"

"You come running in *to act*. You know in advance where and how things will happen. Why do you run into the tavern? To communicate important news to Philip Stepanovich! Do you know where he is sitting? The inn is large. There are many people. Well, sir, what will you do? And the rhythm! The *rhythm!* Why such bullish rhythm? Terrible! Well, once more. Ah, ah, ah."

And the whole four-hour rehearsal was spent on working out my running in. Having achieved what he wanted, Konstantin Sergeyevich ended the rehearsal. We had gone through only one scene.

The following day was the second and last rehearsal of *The Embezzlers*. Stanislavski could not stop a long time on separate moments of the play, but I felt how attentively he watched me during the whole rehearsal and that evening at the play. After the performance I was told that Konstantin Sergeyevich had requested me to see him at the hotel the following day.

After greeting me courteously and affectionately in his hotel room, Konstantin Sergeyevich said with some embarrassment.

"Well, my dear fellow, you forgot everything I taught you. What you did was terrible. It was a return to the old ways."

"I got a little bit off key at the rehearsal, Konstantin Sergeyevich, and that's why yesterday in the performance it somehow didn't come out right, but before that in Moscow I was successful enough and the audience liked me."

"It is very sad that you understand art in this way. The public may like *anything*. Someone called me on the telephone incognito. He was horrified at your acting."

I did not know at that time that "incognito" was simply a trick which Konstantin Sergeyevich used as a way of influencing an actor. He invented this incognito, this person without prejudice, as a balance to himself, who was perhaps too fastidious.

In a very long conversation he explained the important difference between what was in the role and what I had made of it.

"Formerly you found in the role its uninterrupted, organic line-of-action and went along it from event to event, striving for your objective; the public reacted to individual, especially successful moments. You then turned your attention to those moments, seized them and began to underline them. You grew fond of them, their intonations, their mise en scènes, and ignored all the rest; you waited with impatience for those moments where you won cheap laurels, and, of course, the role degenerated, it fell apart, lost its wholeness, its purpose. Earlier it seemed to you that you were playing insipidly. Perhaps that was true, but you were playing truthfully. You ought to have fixed what had been found truthfully and strengthened the through-line-of-action of the role instead of chasing after separate effects. Genuine brilliance could spring from that, but you went in the opposite direction altogether. Don't forget what I am saying to you: Most of all, avoid this untrue path, this path of playing separate pieces, bits, of winning cheap applause in the middle of scenes and at your exits. Regard the role as one entity. Let the audience follow the development of the logic of your conflict, interest them in your fate, so that, not taking their eyes off you, they follow you fearing not only to applaud but to make even the smallest movement which could hinder them from observing all the subtlety of your behavior. This is the playing of an artist; it does not entertain, it reaches deeply into the heart of the audience."

Between the two main productions in which I was privileged to work under the leadership of Stanislavsk, I met with him from time to time—now simply for conversation, now observing his work on plays in which I had no part. Once I was told that Konstantin Sergeyevich would revive Chekhov's *The Cherry Orchard* and had asked that I be present at rehearsals because I would double with I. M. Moskvin in the role of Epikhodov. This news would have excited me at any time, but it did so especially then.

Some twenty years before, during Lent, the Moscow Art Theatre had come on a guest tour to Petersburg and I happened to go, for the first time, to its production of *The Cherry Orchard*. My impression of that performance has already been described. After the play, I went to the theatre club on Lityenie Avenue, the usual meeting place of actors. But that night the usual club entertainment, the gambling table or buffet bar, did not interest me. I wanted to stay alone and think over what I had just seen at the theatre. Sitting in an armchair in one of the cozy rooms of the club, I did not notice that an idol of the public, Y. M. Yuryev, a magnificent artist and a man of rare qualities, had entered. Although he had a somewhat reserved manner, Yuri Mikhailovich was gentle and

kind; he was very warm toward me in particular. I was told
that he had had a very flattering opinion of my examination
performance at the Alexandrinsky Theatre, which had
crowned my theatrical education. And now his exceptionally
pleasant, velvety voice took me out of my reverie.

"What are you thinking about?"

He sat down beside me, and we got into a conversation. In
the pleasant semi-darkness of the room, with its comfortable,
soft armchairs, our conversation lasted until dawn. We began
with the Moscow Art Theatre. Yuri Mikhailovich shared my
enthusiasm for its art, but, all the same, in some ways criticized it while strongly defending the traditions of his beloved
Alexandrinsky Theatre and Moscow's Maly Theatre. We
talked about our art in general, about the technique of the
actor, of his creative difficulties. Yuri Mikhailovich was one of
the representatives of the theatre of that time who constantly
and persistently worked on themselves in order to perfect
their art. He considered work to be the only reliable help in,
at least, approaching dramatic heights. Before parting at
dawn, I once more poured out my stream of enthusiasm for
The Cherry Orchard and especially for Moskvin, who had
played the role of Epikhodov so brilliantly, and complained a
little about my own prospects. Bidding me good-bye and
shaking my hand, Yuri Mikhailovich said: "My dear friend, you
need not worry about your fate as an actor; you are, without
doubt, gifted. Start working and you will soon be noticed; you
will be able to choose a theatre to your liking and in some
twenty years, you will see, you will come to us on a guest tour
of the Moscow Art Theatre troupe. You yourself will play the
part of Epikhodov, and I will applaud you."

At that time I took those words of Yuri Mikhailovich as his
habitual kindness, but still they made me feel happy and
warm.

I remembered this when I was doubling with Moskvin and
especially recalled it when I later went to Leningrad and
played Epikhodov. This was about twenty years after my

conversation with Yuri Mikhailovich in the theatre club on Lityenie Avenue.

Reviving *The Cherry Orchard*, Konstantin Sergeyevich, as always, strove to get rid of the clichés which had accumulated in the actors' performances. But this time he did more than that and, it seemed to me, tried to revise somewhat the original interpretation of the play, eradicating the smallest traces of sentimentality which remained, trying to look at the events in a more contemporary manner. He succeeded in this only partially. The deadline for the production and some resistance on the part of the actors prevented him from fulfilling this task completely.

Moskvin rehearsed the role of Epikhodov; when he was absent I would try to rehearse some of it, but this was without Konstantin Sergeyevich. He did not have time to work with me, the more so because he himself was playing Gaev. Occasionally when I came to his attention he would offer me some material for reflection on the role.

"Bear in mind: if you try to *play* a fool, nothing will come out. He imagines himself a passionate Spaniard, very cultured, but his face . . ."

Here he raised the tip of his finger to his nose, making an unbelievably stupid face.

"And don't play tricks; play Epikhodov as a very serious, cultured man. It is true he is somewhat awkward, he cannot walk without bumping into something, without overturning something. But he looks at his blunders as phenomena of fate, with which it is senseless to struggle, and at which one can only smile."

When I played Epikhodov the first time, Konstantin Sergeyevich inspected my makeup before the beginning of the play, gave me some last-minute advice, and whenever he could, watched me during the play. In the first act there is a wonderful piece of directing: everyone has gone out to meet Ranesvkaya; the stage is empty. From afar comes the jingle of the bells of the approaching carriage, the distant voices of people; then, the meeting between those arriving and those greeting them, joyful cries, laughter, kisses, etc. At the beginning, all these sounds are hardly audible, then, as the actors draw nearer, they become louder and louder until, finally, the excited Ranevskaya runs onto the stage with all the others following. After this everything onstage follows the author's text. That entire scene backstage was the result of the great imagination and the persistent work of the director and made an enchanting impression on the audience. The effect was achieved in the following way: The actors taking part in this scene at first are placed at a distance backstage on a stairway hidden behind an iron stage door. As the scene develops, this door is slightly opened, then it is opened wider and wider until it is completely open; the actors cross the threshold and move in a crowd toward the stage, the whole time acting out the arrival of Ranevskaya and her party; finally, they come onstage and the play proceeds.

Playing Epikhodov for the first time, I was, because of the excitement, a little confused and when I approached the iron door to the stair I found it already closed and all the other actors behind it. I was afraid to open it and remained there, alone, until they should open the door. When I came on with the others, Konstantin Sergeyevich looked askance at me and, at the end of the act, called me to his dressing room and asked:

"Why weren't you in your place?"

"Excuse me, out of excitement I got lost backstage."

"But, finding yourself on the other side of the iron door, did you take part in the general scene?"

"Yes, yes, of course, Konstantin Sergeyevich," I lied.

"Terrible! You spoiled our scene. Oh! Oh! Oh! In the first place, how could you play the scene with us without seeing us? Besides, there is a difference in sound: we were behind the iron door, our voices were muffled; you were out there, your voice sounded completely different. That is false. The scene is subtle, built entirely of nuances, and you destroyed them."

I stood there in confusion.

"On the whole, you do not play badly. But why, in the very first exit, did you stumble on the threshold? In order to show at once that you are a comedian? Why this label? The role must develop gradually. It is much better if the audience takes you at the beginning for a serious man; it is much more advantageous for you. Developing the role, revealing to the audience newer and newer facets of it, you will hold their attention all the time. Why impose upon the audience immediately that you are a comic character, that you will make them laugh today? They will find out for themselves who you are. It is your job to follow the through-line-of-action in all seriousness; then your humor will not be the humor of buffoonery, but the genuine humor of high comedy."

Much later, when I was already sure of the part and had played Epikhodov more than once, a rehearsal was held in Stanislavski's home in Leontyev Lane. One of the young actors was being introduced in the role of Dunyasha or Yasha or Charlotta, I don't remember which. They showed Konstantin Sergeyevich the beginning of the second act where Epikhodov, Yasha, Dunyasha and Charlotta are sitting in a meadow talking. We played the whole scene through. Konstantin Sergeyevich was silent for a long time, and then he said:

"It seems to me that you do not completely understand with what genius this scene is written. Do you appreciate what a group Chekhov has brought together? The very combination of participants, if you think about it, cannot fail to arouse laughter. In it there is a world of humor. Just think about the foolish, well-fed, healthy, country girl Dunyasha, who imagines herself a sickly, delicate, refined young lady. Near her are her two jealous lovers: one a clumsy, ridiculous ignoramus, assured of his culture and learning—a fatalist. The other, a young country booby, who, because he has spent several years in Paris, considers himself a French aristocrat—a marquis at the very least. In addition to them, there is a German governess, a former circus equestrienne, a performer at fairs, an eccentric person who speaks Russian poorly. Each one tries to make a show of his own qualities before the others: one, delicacy of feeling and experience; another, refinement of manners; the third, culture and importance; the fourth, the diversity of her extremely interesting life. No one wants to listen to, or even acknowledge, the others; each one thinks only of himself. Each has an active task: to win the general attention, to belittle the virtues of the others, to force them to listen to him. Moreover, the whole scene is complicated by a tangled love intrigue among Yasha, Dunyasha and Epikhodov. Here is the genuine humor, the genius of Chekhov. How should you approach this? How should you play this scene? Here is the truth of life. Chekhov's fine art lies in his ability to lead us to the very brink of farce without falling into caricature. Following his own logical line, each actor in this scene must be absolutely serious, convinced of his own importance. The more seriously the struggle between the two rivals is carried out—using both subtle, diplomatic means and direct threats, as with the revolver—the nearer you come to Chekhov. Only don't spend yourself on small tricks, do not turn this high work of art into trite commonplaceness; be strict with yourself as an artist. Such was Chekhov; that's why his work reaches the highest quality of humor."

The meetings with Stanislavski which introduced the work on *Dead Souls* did not leave any special impressions on my memory; they were not numerous and not very significant. On the other hand, from the moment when work on *Dead Souls* began, up to its end, each rehearsal, each conversation with him is firmly rooted in my consciousness, and sometimes small details of our relationship come to the surface with such clarity that they seem to have happened only yesterday.

The work on the part of Chichikov was the most important milestone of my artistic life. With it, finally, I began to gain an understanding of those elements in Stanislavski's system which until that time had been unclear to me. This didn't come at once. I followed a difficult path, I suffered a great deal, experienced many shocks, great failures and disappointments, but nothing weakened my faith in the rightness of the way shown me by Stanislavski. Although this way did not lead me to success in my first performances in that part, nevertheless, it finally led me to the road I had been seeking since my school days. In search of this, I had had to wander long and agonizingly in the darkness.

Dead Souls

V. G. SAKHNOVSKY, the director who prepared *Dead Souls*, wrote in the October 15, 1932, issue of *Soviet Art:*

"The work of Konstantin Sergeyevich with the actors on scenes from *Dead Souls* forms one of the most remarkable chapters in the history of the Moscow Art Theatre. Some rehearsals of ours have been written down in their entirety, some in part, but these rehearsals will remain in the memory of all the participants not only as examples of remarkable directing of actors coping with the characters of Gogol, but as indications of new methods in working on a role. At some rehearsals, the actors unrestrainedly applauded Konstantin Stanislavski when he revealed new ideas which completely changed their reactions to familiar things."

Indeed, forced to perform a miracle by the special circumstances that accompanied the production of this play, Konstantin Sergeyevich mobilized all his powers, all his directorial mastery in a way which could not help but astonish those present at the rehearsals.

In those not so distant times, many of our theatres were still in the grip of a reactionary formalism. In search of the greatest expressiveness and in an attempt to present "ideological trends," they got lost in paths of vulgar sociology, presenting the authors' concepts in sharp forms of exaggeration which were called by the then-fashionable name "grotesque." There was a kind of directorial orgy. There was much sincere enthusiasm on the part of talented but confused directors, especially among the young, as well as naïve imitation of mediocre, dilettante directors. There were also adroit adventurers who took advantage of this state of confusion.

One could write a long entertaining book by just enumerating all the absurdities and curious things about their attempts at innovation. Harmonious, monumental works of our great classic dramatists were sliced into small episodes, and out of these, works were made which reminded one of a patchwork quilt. At the whim of the director characters were distorted beyond recognition, regardless of the intentions of the author. In one of Ostrovsky's plays, *The League of Nations*, for no reason the actors often climbed onto a trapeze, walked a tightrope, etc.

"Aesthetic" theatre critics, naturally, were on the side of the innovators. They attacked everything which had the least trace of wholesome ideas of theatre art. It was clear that their arrows were directed mainly at the Moscow Art Theatre, which was trying not only to preserve its realistic traditions but also to develop them along modern lines, to which such a production as Ivanov's *Armored Train 14–69* bears witness.

Sakhnovsky began the work on Gogol cautiously but with a tendency toward the grotesque. I do not know what part Stanislavski or Nemirovich-Danchenko played at the beginning of the work, but in any case they were not present at rehearsals.

Sakhnovsky, a director of special individuality and personality, at that time was only beginning to become familiar with the Moscow Art Theatre, and his indefatigable striving for stage expressiveness was not yet sufficiently attuned to the theatre's practice. A highly educated man, a very interesting conversationalist, he thought and spoke in magnificent, brilliant paradoxes, and his method of working with actors bore a somewhat paradoxical character. It did not have the concreteness of a professional director; his was more of a literary and philosophical approach. In his effort to penetrate into the inner meaning of Gogol's work, we were made to do all kinds of things which were, unfortunately, not of practical use.

Sakhnovsky carried on endless conversations with us, which consisted of very witty speculations about Gogol's personality, about his world outlook and his relationship with his contemporaries, etc. We visited museums to look at portraits of Gogol, studied his works, his letters, his biography. In order to emphasize the fact that we were trading in dead souls, Sakhnovsky once suggested that I go to the cemetery. What Sakhnovsky said would always be interesting, fascinating and more or less true, but not sufficiently concrete. No matter how many times we went to the cemeteries, museums and picture galleries, no matter how many times we carried on fascinating, stimulating conversations, all these proved to be only superfluous baggage for our practical work. We worked, all the same, with great enthusiasm; now finding something, now losing it. But for the most part, we worked without any exact reference point. Then we arrived at the general rehearsal to which Stanislavski came.

I will not describe the rehearsal in detail; I will say only that Konstantin Sergeyevich became completely bewildered. He told the directors that he had understood nothing of what he had seen, that we had come to an impasse and would have to throw it all out and begin all over again.

I did not hear what Konstantin Sergeyevich said to the directors and the others who had taken part in this work, therefore I can only recount what was said from information given me by the participants and by Konstantin Sergeyevich himself. However, reconstructing in my memory the details of Stanislavski's work on *Dead Souls*, the directions that he gave in the course of the rehearsals, I think I can indicate how he saved the play.

Without doubt, the first task Stanislavski had was to find the dramatic core of this imperfect dramatic work. On what should he build the plot line of the play? To what should the audience's attention be directed? There had been more than a hundred dramatizations of Gogol's poem, but not one of them had met with any success. Their dramatic looseness was the cause. In old times, separate scenes from *Dead Souls* had been played and had enjoyed great success. However, as soon as these separate scenes were put together into a whole play, the repetition of the same subject—the buying of dead souls—without being linked to a central core could not hold the attention of the audiences. In the middle of the performance the audience began to be bored, in spite of such wonderful actors as Varlamov, Davydov or Dalmatov.

The most thankless part in those dramatizations was the remarkable character Chichikov, so wonderfully depicted by Gogol. He appears throughout the entire play, but as he is limited to repeating almost literally one and the same thing from scene to scene, he quickly bores the audience, the more so since around him are a whole gallery of very diverse, colorful Gogol types—landowners, peasants and officials.

But on Chichikov Stanislavski decided to build the plot line of the play. With this aim in mind, the staging was somewhat altered and the work of Stanislavski with the actors took a direction in accordance with it.

"The Career of Chichikov", this must be the theme of the play, this is what the audience must follow. So Konstantin Sergeyevich decided. Does this mean that Stanislavski limited the play to this task only? Certainly not. He took the laws of the theatre well into account and knew that the more perfect a play is in its dramatic aspect, the more reliable a conductor of ideas it will be. If a play is imperfect, it is the task of the director to perfect it; not by the addition of embellishments which take the audience's attention from the essence of the play, but by strengthening its through-line-of-action.

At one of the rehearsals Konstantin Sergeyevich said:

"What shall we do with Chichikov? How are we to escape these invariable and monotonous arrivals and conversations

always about the same thing? They can be made interesting
only by following the through-line-of-action. We must manage
to show how Chichikov's plan to purchase dead serfs arises
from a chance shock; how this plan expands, grows, rises to its
height and finally collapses completely. If you can grasp the
through-line-of-action in this role—honor and praise to you.
But it will be very difficult."

The task *was* difficult, in general and in detail. Having
chosen Chichikov as the leading character in the plot line of
the play, Stanislavski discovered that he did not have an actor
adequate for the role. My stage gifts could perhaps have
approached the grotesque Chichikov we unfortunately had
tried to embody until the intervention of Stanislavski, but I
could not touch the authentic Chichikov of Gogol's poem.
Moreover, our previous attempts to twist the Gogol character
into a grotesque, to substitute a mask in place of a living face,
to sharpen an image which was already perfectly sharp, naturally distorted in me any idea of the truth, of anything human
and organic; my genuine flair and motivation toward creativity was paralyzed.

The current theatre mode which had prompted us to take
a false position toward the work in those first rehearsals had
led us to a creative impasse from which only a person of great
practical experience could free us.

"All your joints are dislocated," said Stanislavski to me
after that dress rehearsal. "You do not have one whole limb
left; first, you need to have all your bones reset and learn to
walk again; not to *play*, just to walk!"

Konstantin Sergeyevich called only me to the first rehearsals in order to correct my "dislocated joints." He worked with
me attentively and carefully, like a doctor with a patient, and
as I look back on it now, I see that the work proceeded chiefly
by organizing and modeling the organic line of the physical
behavior of Chichikov. This way of proceeding, which he
afterward advanced as a more truthful way of mastering the
stage character in its full measure, later received the name
"the method of physical actions."

The work began with conversations, but conversations which had nothing in common with those which we had had with Sakhnovsky earlier. Stanislavski pulled us down from the clouds. The questions he asked astounded us with their simplicity, lucidity, concreteness. I was even somewhat disappointed and perplexed: this was all *too* simple, *too* commonplace and far from those objectives which we envisioned. Moreover, our previous work had dimmed my brain so much that I had difficulty in answering even the simplest questions.

"Are you able to bargain?" Stanislavski asked me.

"What do you mean 'bargain?' "

"Well, to buy something cheap, to sell it for more, to be able to throw dust in the buyer's eyes, to praise your own goods and to discredit the goods of the seller, to guess his lowest price, to pretend to be poorer, to swear, to take a vow, etc."

"No, I'm no good at that."

"You need to learn how; it is most important for your part."

"Why, after all, does Chichikov buy the dead?," Konstantin Sergeyevich asked me unexpectedly.

What might one answer? It is evident to everyone, but . . .

"Well, for what purpose?"

"Gogol writes that he will mortgage the dead serfs as living and receive money for them."

"And what for?"

"What do you mean, 'what for?' "

"Why is this advantageous to him; what does he need the money for? What will he do with it? Have you thought of that?"

"No, I haven't thought in such detail."

"Well, think about it."

A long pause.

"When the souls have been mortgaged and the money received, what then?"

Again, a pause.

"You should know the final goal of all this exactly and in much greater detail than you do. Think it through thoroughly and study the whole life of Chichikov in order to collect material for your practical work on the role."

Konstantin Sergeyevich very delicately, very skillfully led me to ideas, but he never thrust anything upon me ready-made. He simply excited my imagination.

"Put yourself in Chichikov's place. What would you do under such circumstances?"

"Yes, but I am not Chichikov; I am not interested in gain."

"Well, if you *were* a bit interested, how would you act?"

In these conversations the simplest things were decided, but they touched upon the most urgent aspects of Chichikov's life. There was nothing of that dark obstruseness which the representatives of today's militant formalism are so fond of. Andrea Beli, who directed his sharply critical article, "Misunderstood Gogol", against our production, wrote: "Some more observations about the symbolism of details in Gogol's text: *Dead Souls* begins with the description of Chichikov's carriage. The peasants who happened to be present at his arrival exchanged remarks about one of its wheels. Among the 'souls' sold to Chichikov by Korobochka, who played such a fatal part in the unmasking of this hero, was one peasant by the name of Ivan Koleso [wheel]; at the moment of Chichikov's flight from the provincial capital it was discovered that the *wheel* of the carriage was damaged."

I mention this excerpt only to show that such symbolic detail did not interest Stanislavski in the work on *Dead Souls*. Such examination of the text he counted as nonsense. On the contrary, it was the simple, real troubles and deeds of the poem's hero that interested him.

How much money did Chichikov have when he gave the bribe to the Guardian Council, how big was this bribe, etc. In short, he required the smallest details of the life of his hero. All these questions I had to answer myself. So I attempted to resolve them while waiting for work on the part to begin, not understanding that in doing this the work had already begun, although in a way that was unusual for me.

The moment when we turned from conversation to action passed somehow imperceptibly.

PROLOGUE

Here is the text of the Prologue of our dramatization of *Dead Souls;* the scene is in a room at an inn in the capital.

CHICHIKOV: Mister Secretary!

SECRETARY: Mister Chichikov! You again? What does this mean? In the morning you plague me in the Council, in the evening you catch me here at the inn. Let me pass! I have told you already, my good fellow, that I cannot do anything for you.

CHICHIKOV: As you wish, your Honor, but I am not leaving until I receive a satisfactory decision from you. My employer is going away . . .

SECRETARY: Your employer ruined his estate.

CHICHIKOV: Numberless as the sands of the sea are human passions, Most Honorable.

SECRETARY: Indeed numberless. He went on a spree, lost at cards, ruined himself completely. Your employer's estate is in the worst possible condition and you want to mortgage it to the Guardian Council for two hundred rubles a serf! Who will take that as security?

CHICHIKOV: Why are you so strict, your Excellency? The estate was ruined by a severe loss of cattle, by bad harvests, by a rogue of a steward.

SECRETARY: Hm!

CHICHIKOV (*Taking out a bribe and handing it to the* SECRETARY): You dropped this, sir.

SECRETARY: But I am not the only one on the Council; there are others.

CHICHIKOV: The others will not be forgotten. I myself have been a functionary; I know all about it.

SECRETARY: Good, send in the papers.

CHICHIKOV: By the way, there is something else you should know in order to avoid any complications later: half the peasants on the estate have died.

SECRETARY *(Laughing)*: What an estate! Not only is it ruined but the people are dead.

CHICHIKOV: Well, your Excellency ...

SECRETARY: Well, according to the inspector's report they were counted as living.

CHICHIKOV: Counted as living?

SECRETARY: Well, what are you frightened about? One dies, another is born—everything fits. According to the inspector's report they were counted as living so they must be considered alive.

CHICHIKOV: But ...

SECRETARY: What?

CHICHIKOV: Nothing.

SECRETARY: Well, then? Submit the papers. *(He goes out.)*

CHICHIKOV: Ah, what a fool I am—like Akim the Simple! Here I am looking for my pencil and it is stuck behind my ear! Of course! I will buy all those who have died before the lists have been submitted to the inspector.... If I buy, let us say, a thousand, and then mortgage them to the Guardian Council at two hundred rubles a soul—there is already two hundred thousand rubles of capital! Ah, but without land one cannot either buy or mortgage. *(With inspiration)* Land in Khersonsky province is being given for nothing if you populate it! I will move them all there, the dead ones—to Khersonsky province! To the province! Let their corpses live there. The times are propitious now: not long ago there was an epidemic and many people died. Thank God, a *great* many. Under the pretext of settling people there, I will visit places where it will be easy and cheap to buy the necessary "souls." First, a visit to the Governor. Of course, it will be difficult and troublesome. It is frightening to consider what will happen if I am caught: publicly lashed and perhaps even sent to Siberia.... Well, isn't intelligence given to man for some purpose? The main advantage is that no one will believe it. The thing will appear

incredible to everyone. No one will believe it. . . . I am going, I
am going!

(*Blackout*)

After a series of catastrophes on his employer's estate,
Chichikov finds himself no better off than when he started;
everything seems quite hopeless. With, figuratively, a noose
around his neck, he is about to undertake a very dubious
venture—to mortgage an almost completely destroyed estate
on which more than half the serfs have died. To do so, he must
get the help of the Secretary of the Guardian Council, an arch
scoundrel who could not be wound around one's finger.
Chichikov has already plagued him by his importunity and the
opportunities to bribe him have become more and more limited. But the man whom bankruptcy and destitution threatens
is ready for anything. In this scene, Chichikov, like a blood-
hound, comes upon the track of the Secretary, finds him in the
inn and decides either to gain his end or die.

All this was discussed with Stanislavski as a starting point
for understanding Chichikov's behavior in the Prologue of the
play.

"Now, how would you act under the given circumstances.
Vasily Osipovich?"

"I think that here Chichikov feels . . ."

"Don't think of that, think of how he *acts*. Well, then?"

A pause.

"Your partner, Vsevolod Alexeyevich, is sitting here before
you. How he will respond to you is very important. Now try
before everything else to make yourself more at ease with him.
By the look in his eyes, determine what you may count on; do
not *think*, try to *act* immediately."

After several attempts, when it seemed as if something was
beginning to come, Konstantin Sergeyevich continued:

"Well, what if he refuses to listen to you and goes out? Go
out, Vsevolod Alexeyevich, do not listen, do not pay any
attention to him. You, Vasily Osipovich, hold him, but not

with your hands, do it without using physical force, only do not allow him to go. . . . No, that way he will get away."

"I don't know what I must do!"

"In life if you needed him very much, you would find a way to hold him; why can't you do it here? It is a simple thing, the simplest exercise. The task consists only of this: One of you gets up from the chair unexpectedly and goes to the door; the other must nip his intention in the bud; he must stop him, not allowing him to go beyond a certain point. This is very simple. Now try, only don't *perform;* be natural, be really interested in what you are doing."

I was acquainted with this exercise from our previous work on *The Embezzlers,* and I will not enumerate here all the subtleties Stanislavski employed to get live, organic behavior from me in this scene. I will only say that the work was long and painstaking and was concerned only with physical behavior.

"Here you just learn to do a series of physical actions. Join them in one unbroken line, then you will have the scheme of the physical actions of the Prologue. In essence what do you have to do here? You sit in ambush and follow the smallest movement of your partner. The moment he makes an attempt to go out, stop him, skillfully block his way, interest him in something, surprise him, confuse him. Take advantage of this and palm off the bribe so that no one around will notice. This is enough for the present. This is a very important introductory part of the Prologue. Learn to do it well. If you must use words for this, please do not use the author's exact text, only the ideas embodied in it. Don't *act* anything, just play each action. Don't do anything for us, do everything only for your partner. Check, through your partner's reaction, if you are acting well."

In the second part of the Prologue, which properly leads to the monologue of Chichikov beginning with the words "Ah, what a fool I am—like Akim . . . ," Konstantin Sergeyevich again traced the line of physical actions, notwithstanding that here it would seem there were no physical actions. Chichikov is sitting at a table while he delivers the monologue.

"This is not a monologue, but a dialogue. There is a hot argument here between reason and feeling. Separate these two 'partners'—one of them is in the head, the other somewhere in the solar plexus—then let them communicate with each other. Depending upon which gains the upper hand, Chichikov either attempts to jump up from the table and run out to accomplish the shady transaction before 'they' grab his idea, or he tries with all his strength to hold himself on the chair. You feel, you understand these urges to action; try to carry them out."

Until a certain point, everything revolved around purely physical behavior. This led to very different methods of study—the variety of actions was significantly greater than in the work on *The Embezzlers*. Following this method, the work took on the form of entertaining play: either that of a lesson, where we practiced the elements of the simplest physical actions and where Stanislavski turned into the most pedantic, fault-finding pedagogue, or that of improvisation, where we improvised the behavior of the characters in the Prologue with words. This work continued until the given task was carried out by us in such measure that we could satisfactorily recount and perform the physical action of the Prologue.

At that time I still did not comprehend the deep meaning of this work. I did not know Konstantin Sergeyevich's secret: that through the correct execution of physical actions, through their logic and their sequence, one penetrates into the deepest, most complicated feelings and emotional experiences; that is, one finally reaches the very qualities which we had tried so unsuccessfully to achieve in the first period of our work. At that time neither Konstantin Sergeyevich nor we actors spoke or thought about exalted objectives but worked on the solution of the simplest stage tasks and tried to achieve the greatest perfection in their fulfillment. And so imperceptibly, step by step, we came to the moment when the author's text was necessary, when there arose the desire to use it. Here I was, standing before my partner and saying:

"As you wish, Excellency, but I will not leave until I get a proper decision from you."

Suddenly several hand claps and the sweet, apologetic voice of Stanislavski:

"I am sorry, I don't understand what you were saying."

"As you wish, Excellency, but I will not leave . . ."

"Excuse me, I don't understand anything. What 'Excellency?' "

"As you wish, Excellency . . ."

"What! As you wish?"

"As you wish, Excellency, but I will not leave this place . . ."

"I am sorry, excuse me, I somehow cannot understand anything. H'm . . . H'm . . . Maybe it's my sclerosis. I am beginning to hear badly." Then, addressing the directors, "What is in the text?"

The directors with the utmost clarity try to pronounce the sentence, but Konstantin Sergeyevich does not change his blank expression. I even become somehow sorry for him and I start to speak very carefully. With the utmost expressiveness I say:

"As you wish, Excellency, but I will not leave until I get a proper decision from you."

"Ah, now I understand. Speak as clearly to your partner. You must convince a man who does not want to listen to you. Do you feel how there must be energy in all your actions? Well, now go on."

I repeated the sentence.

"Horrible. What is that? You hit every word: *"Aś yóu wish, Eẍcellenćy, bút I wíll nót leáve untíl I ġet á propér decision from ẏou.'* If you do that, the sentence will lose all its vitality. The meaning is clearest when, regardless of the length of a sentence, there is only one main stress. Earlier you had a real desire that I should understand your meaning, but just now you began to *act* instead of playing your actions. Well, once more, please. . . . Horrible! Where is the stress in this sentence? Which single word would be enough for the scene to be understood? Without which word would you not be able to get what you need from your partner?

"What do you want from him? What must he do to satisfy you? The answer is already in the sentence itself! What are you thinking of? You even say that you will not leave this place, until . . . what?"

"Until I receive . . ."

"Well?"

"The decision."

"Yes, *that* is the main accented word. You must give the single stress in the whole sentence only on that word."

I say the line, trying to give it only one stress.

"But why do you jumble the rest of the words? You don't have to hurry or mumble them, just don't stress them. Well, then . . ."

Again I say it.

"Why so much emphasis on the last word?"

"What do you mean 'so much emphasis?' "

"Why do you push de-ci-sion?"

"But the accent is on that!"

"Yes, but not so strong. You only need to take the emphasis from all the rest, then the single accent will remain. Well, now . . ."

When the uninitiated were present at such especially difficult moments during Stanislavski's rehearsals, it often seemed to them grotesque: "Here is the usual actors' exaggeration. Really! It is too much to harass people so. Where is the personal creativity? Such torture of an actor cannot lead to anything good, it only confuses him." Actually, after two or three hours' work on one sentence you sometimes stop understanding the meaning of the words, or so it seems. But only temporarily. Later, on the contrary, the meaning of the sentences and words becomes especially clear; having gone through such "purifying fire," you begin to regard the sentence into which you have put so much effort with a special respect. You will not mumble it, nor will you clutter it with unnecessary stresses. It becomes musical and effective.

Can an actor be so exacting toward himself? Can he work so insistently on the perfecting of his technique? Hardly. Because, above all, he really does not see or hear himself; he does not understand his shortcomings. All the bad habits which have clung to the actor through the years hold on tenaciously. To remove them, great patience and courage are demanded as well as help from people of authority to whom the laws of creativity are well known. This is why we never complained about the overcaptiousness of Konstantin Sergeyevich; the great attainments of the Moscow Art Theatre could never have been reached if the actors had not gone through the strenuous school of Stanislavski.

But to return to the rehearsal. Stanislavski considered *action* the undeniable and sole basis of the actor's art. Everything else he ruthlessly eliminated. "Why do you do that?" "What does that contribute to the through-line-of-action?" Everything that did not lead to the achievement of the objective, to the superobjective, was held unnecessary.

Every physical action must be active, must lead to the attainment of some kind of objective. This holds true, too, for every sentence spoken on the stage. Stanislavski often cited the ingenious saying: "Your words will not be empty nor your silences dumb."

For the sharpening of verbal action, Stanislavski had many teaching methods. But they could all be divided into two categories: one, the outer line, studying the logical construction of the sentence; the other, the inner line, developing in the actor images which he can justify, of graphic representations which underlie the text of the role. I have already given an example of the outer line: "As you wish, Excellency, etc." There Konstantin Sergeyevich made sure that the actor learned to give only one stress in long sentences on the most important word, thus making it more active and more effective.

"You are given a role which consists of ideas, all of which reach toward the most important one, and all of which are colored by it."

The actor's task in verbal action consists in imparting his own images to his partner. In order to do this, he must see very clearly what he is talking about. If he does this, his partner, too, will see through the "inner window" the picture drawn for him clearly and in detail.

From concentration on the verbal action and the images which underlie it, we proceeded to the second part of the Prologue of *Dead Souls*, the concluding monologue of Chichikov.

"Ah, what a fool I am—like Akim the Simple." Having dashingly read through the monologue and having slammed my fist very effectively on the table with the last words, "I am going," I got up from the table and glanced triumphantly at Konstantin Sergeyevich.

"Hm! . . . Hm! . . . Nothing! My dear fellow, you don't see *anything.*"

A pause.

"You say words . . . you see in them letters as they are written in a notebook, not the images beneath them."

"I don't understand."

"Here, for instance, you said, 'publicly lashed and perhaps even sent to Siberia.' You should see in those words the picture of execution, flogging, a halting place for convicts, severe Siberia. This is most important. Now then, begin once more."

"Ah, what a fool . . . Akim . . ."

"You don't *see.* You just say *words.* First, accumulate images; see yourself in Akim the Simple; then, scold yourself because you are such a simpleton. What is this Akim the Simple? How do you see him? Well, then, please!"

"Ah, what a fool . . ."

"Dreadful! Hm! At once—voltage. You try to agitate your-self outwardly, to call forth nervous tension and to overload everything. You are in a fog. You should simply concentrate; see clearly where you blundered and scold yourself soundly. That's all. Now!"

"Ah . . ."

"Why 'ah?' Not 'ah,' but 'Ah . . . I, Akim the Simple.' Where is the accented word here? Once you have a false stress, you do not see what you are talking about."

And again a whole new rehearsal crisis was created.

Finally out of the chaos of details, of separate outlines accumulated in the rehearsals, the plot of the entire play began to be visible. Then it became clear to me that Konstantin Sergeyevich wanted the play to begin immediately to sound vigorous, powerful and musical. By means of these preliminary studies, he had been trying to bring this about. It was important to him to saturate our actions with the sharpest rhythms. He knew that one does not grasp this at once, that it has to develop in an actor; that one must lay out channels through which the stream of the actor's temperament may flow. When this work had been made clear, Stanislavski found it possible to talk about "the result."

"The Prologue," he used to say, "is the tuning fork for the whole play. Do you feel what a responsibility lies in this? What is needed here? Only attention, concentration, good, clear images and the feeling of truth. Here at the table you must watch the Secretary of the Guardian Council carefully so that he may not leave the inn. Your life depends on this. Feel what rhythm is here, what thoughts. You must be ready at any second to spring ten or fifteen feet to block the Secretary's way to the door. Pay attention to this simple physical action. Your first words to him: 'I am not leaving . . .' must make this image clear to him, so that he sees plainly that you will raise a scandal in the inn if he takes it into his head to oppose you. 'I am not leaving . . .' Do you see what this means?

"Further, when you have achieved this, and he has entered into conversation with you, you have to contrive a way to give the bribe so that no one in the inn will see. Then if the Secretary attempts to hold you responsible later, it will be easier to deny everything. Besides this, the whole business must be finished quickly, because tomorrow the head of the Council is going away. When, like a drop of poison, the intriguing idea of buying dead souls comes into his mind, Chichikov must decide at a moment's notice about this risky undertaking. This is where your inner images are especially important. Do you understand? On the one hand, public lashing . . . chains . . . Siberia. . . . And on the other . . . two hundred thousand capital, a luxurious estate . . . a wife, children, family, paradise on earth, the realization of all your highest aspirations. It must be now or never—this is what you must see so that your decision will be inwardly justified."

Even after this had been so clearly presented to us, I cannot say that we did not encounter difficulties in our attempts to accomplish the tasks set before us. Not at all. But what was necessary for us to do, what we had to work on, did not seem so obscure. I could begin to tell why this or that was not turning out well and recognize what I had to practice in order to get it right. There are unlimited challenges for an actor in this short scene. But how difficult . . .

But then Stanislavski often said, "Nothing comes without work; only that which is acquired with difficulty is worth anything."

AT THE GOVERNOR'S

This scene takes place immediately after the Prologue. In the Prologue only the decision to act was made by Chichikov; in this scene, the action itself is begun. Here is the beginning of the realization of the plan.

The GOVERNOR, in a dressing gown with a medal around his

neck, is seated at an embroidery frame, singing to himself:

"Believe me, a girl need not be frank with everyone.

"One can fall in love with her, naturally, but how to speak of this?"

SERVANT: Your Excellency, Councilor Paul Ivanovich Chichikov is here to see you.

GOVERNOR: Chichikov? Give me my frock coat! *(Continuing to sing):* "Should one tell you frankly that it is foolish for an old man to fall in love?" *(The* SERVANT *gives him the coat.)* Ask him to come in. *(The* SERVANT *exits).*

CHICHIKOV *(Entering):* Arriving in town, I considered it my duty without fail to pay my respects to its first dignitary; I counted it my duty to present myself in person to your Excellency.

GOVERNOR: Greatly pleased to make your acquaintance. I beg you to be seated. (CHICHIKOV *sits.)* Where do you serve?

CHICHIKOV: My service began in the Federal Chamber. Further work continued in different places. I was with the Construction Commission . . .

GOVERNOR: Construction of what?

CHICHIKOV: The Cathedral of Christ the Savior, in Moscow, your Excellency.

GOVERNOR: Loyal fellow.

CHICHIKOV: What an opportunity! The Cathedral very fortunately came to me when I was working in the Outer Court of the Customs House.

GOVERNOR: In the Customs House?

CHICHIKOV: In general, I am the most insignificant worm in the whole world, but I am the personification of patience. An enemy in my office made an attempt on my life that neither words, colors, nor brush can describe. My life can be likened to a ship on a rough sea, your Excellency.

GOVERNOR: A ship?

CHICHIKOV: A ship, your Excellency.

GOVERNOR: Learned fellow!

CHICHIKOV *(aside):* He *is* a fool, this governor!

GOVERNOR: To what place do you go?

CHICHIKOV: I am looking for a little nook in which to spend the declining years of my life. The remainder is the remainder; to see the light and the mingling of people is already of itself, so to speak, a living book and a second science.

GOVERNOR: Just so! Just so!

CHICHIKOV: In your Excellency's province one moves as in Paradise.

GOVERNOR: Why?

CHICHIKOV: The roads everywhere are like velvet.

(*The* GOVERNOR *grins in embarrassment.*)

Governments which appoint wise officials deserve much praise.

GOVERNOR: Most amiable . . . Paul *Ivan*ovich?

CHICHIKOV: Paul Ivanovich, your Excellency.

GOVERNOR: I beg you to come to my party this evening.

CHICHIKOV: I would esteem it a special honor, your Excellency. I have the honor to bow. Ah, who embroidered this border so skillfully?

GOVERNOR (*bashfully*): Why I am embroidering this purse.

CHICHIKOV: You don't say so! (*He admires it.*) I have the honor . . . (*He steps back and goes out.*)

GOVERNOR: A pleasant fellow! (*He begins to sing.*) "Should I tell you frankly that it is hard to love an old man . . ."

(*Blackout*)

"What then is the link in the long chain of the through-line-of-action of the role of Chichikov? What concrete task does Paul Ivanovich set for himself in making his visit to the Governor? What problem must he resolve in order to proceed? How can he accomplish this? Through what action can he most truthfully attain his objective?" asked Stanislavski.

"For Chichikov, this visit was extremely important. In the first place, in the home of the Governor he could become acquainted with the landowners from whom he could buy his 'goods' in the future, and with the functionaries through whom he could make his deals. It was important that the Governor himself should introduce him into this circle, that he have his recommendation. In order for this all to come about, what did Chichikov have to accomplish during his short visit?

"Now, tell me . . . give me one word, a verb which will intensify your line of action."

"To please the Governor."

"Yes, but be even more exact."

"Well, to flatter him."

"Can we not say 'win?' To *win* his heart. Do you understand?"

"Yes."

"What concrete indications must there be for you to consider your goal 100 percent attained? What will make you feel completely satisfied?

[*A pause.*]

"Did you receive something from the Governor at this visit that furthered your through-line-of-action?"

"Yes."

"What exactly?"

"Well, he was kind to me. He smiled, shook hands . . ."

"As your host, to be polite and amiable, he might have just pretended. Think about it. Why did you want to get into his home?"

"In order to make the acquaintance of the landowners and . . ."

"How will you get into the house of the Governor? In order to get in, what do you need?"

"An invitation."

"And did you receive it?"

"Yes, he said, 'Come to my reception this evening.' "

"That is it, that is the most important, the most concrete thing that you could achieve with your visit. The whole scene is for the sake of this. Everything leads to this, try to achieve only this. This is your task: to obtain an invitation. Well, sir, how will you act?"

"I will speak very civilly with him."

"Then he will say: 'What a fawning fellow this is!' and in three minutes he will dismiss you. In this—indeed, in order to carry out *any* scheme—you must take stock of the person with whom you have to deal. There must be time for a moment of orientation, time in which to feel out your partner. But you decide straight off. When you see the Governor the first time the first thing that you should do, in order not to put your foot in it, is to size up the person before you quickly and then decide how best to approach him. Probably you won't be able to carry on a confident attack for some little while. This first moment of orientation, which in life occurs almost unconsciously, we almost always neglect on the stage. Well then, let us commence."

"I don't know what to do exactly. Read the text?"

"The text is not important, begin to act."

"But my partner . . ."

"I will be your partner. Now then, go out of the room and then come back in as if for the first time. Act in such a way as to make a most pleasant impression on me."

"And the text?"

"Why the text? Let us speak of our affairs. What is important to me is your behavior."

Then persistent work began in the same manner as in the Prologue.

"Well, now, what are you thinking about? In your experience in life did you ever give yourself the task of being pleasing to someone?"

"Yes, but here that didn't work."

"Why?"

"Because a person often thinks one thing but does just the opposite."

"Well, if you did what you thought of doing, would it work then?"

"Yes . . . probably."

"Well, then, do it now. In the Prologue shyness hindered you, but here there is no reason to be shy. Please go on."

Step by step we studied the delicate behavior of a guest who wishes to make a favorable impression on the master of the house. There is the special, noiseless entrance, the feeling of confusion before such an important host, the high regard for his opinions, the modesty of one's own behavior. There is the respectful attitude toward objects in the apartment, museum pieces, and the well thought-out, detailed answers to questions. But most important, in all this there should be sincerity and an absence of any little "mistakes" which might reveal Chichikov's real character. Let the audience, which has not seen the Prologue, take Chichikov for a really decent, humble fellow; had it but seen the Prologue, it would be astonished at the dexterity of this swindler.

"But, Konstantin Sergeyevich, doesn't everything I do in this scene reveal him—his image, his manner?"

"Wait a bit, not so fast. In your work you must start from yourself, from your natural qualities, then follow the laws of creativity. What of Chichikov's manner? Train yourself thoroughly; when you learn to do easily, cleverly and advisedly everything which you already do, then you will really come close to the character."

"But here Gogol has written in a special bow which Chichikov makes."

"Well, what of it?"

"Somehow I cannot make it."

"Did you practice it?"

"Yes, I tried to do it, but it doesn't work out."

"Find a corresponding exercise. For example, mentally place a drop of mercury on the top of your head and then let it roll slowly down your spine to your heel so that it doesn't fall to the floor. Practice this exercise several times a day. Now then, try it. . . . Horrible. Place the mercury on your head. Do you feel it? Wait. Now then, carefully lower your head so that the mercury rolls down the back of your neck . . . now, further along your spine . . . then further and further."

"Arriving in town," I continued to rehearse, "I considered it my duty without fail to pay my respects to its first dignitary; I counted it my duty to present myself in person to your Excellency . . ."

"Hm! Hm! You understand that 'respects to its first dignitary' and 'present myself . . . to your Excellency' are two stressed ideas. 'Your Excellency' is one idea; 'respects to its first dignitary' is the other. Build up this sentence so that 'present myself to your Excellency' is as final as a stone thrown into a chasm."

In this way the tedious work proceeded.

Stanislavski painstakingly molded the Governor's scene in the following way:

After dinner, the Governor is sitting in his study before an embroidery frame, embroidering with delight a design for a purse. He is enraptured with his work and sings loudly and out of key a music-hall song which he had heard somewhere the day before and which had stuck in his memory. Suddenly his servant announces the arrival of Chichikov. The announcement plunges the Governor into deep confusion; he does not want to interrupt his favorite occupation. To refuse? But who is this Chichikov? "I will have to take off my dressing gown and put on my frock coat. . . . But what can I do; the Devil take him! Give me my coat."

The Governor already has come to hate this unknown Chichikov and decides to receive him as distantly as possible. He puts on his dress coat, stands beside the chair and assumes a formal pose.

Chichikov enters. The glances of the Governor and Chichikov meet like two rapiers. This is the moment of orientation for both.

"Well, this one will not joke; he will immediately throw me out!" runs through Chichikov's mind. "It will be just as it was in the army." A Chichikov bow, especially precise and respectful, and then, like a report:

"Arriving in the town, I considered it my duty, etc."

His debut, it seems, was successful. Chichikov is favored with an invitation to sit down, but he is still guarded in his movements. He carefully approaches the table, moves the chair as if unworthy to sit too close to such an exalted person and hesitates for several moments before sitting in the antique armchair. Finally, he sits on the very edge. The Governor asks questions to which Chichikov replies distinctly and respectfully, at first without any fawning. During this time each is

studying and feeling out the other. Each has important motives for this, Chichikov especially. This meeting will decide
his destiny. The Governor begins to consider Chichikov a loyal
and educated person, but Chichikov comes to look on the
Governor as a fool and they both begin to behave toward one
another according to their revised evaluations: the Governor,
with some kindness and respect, Chichikov, shamelessly flattering. The clock strikes. This reminds Chichikov that he must
not take too much of a state official's time. He quickly stands
up and bows with gratitude. Having received the invitation to
the evening party, Chichikov, sincerely happy, bows once
more and starts for the door; but on the way he catches sight
of the embroidery frame. He immediately understands whose
work it is but hesitates as if he cannot take his eyes from it,
seemingly struck by its artistic quality. He forgets the presence of the Governor, forgets all courtesies, and, stunned, he
stands still. Finally, after a long pause, he tears his eyes away
from the embroidery and in astonishment looks at the Governor.

"Who embroidered this border so skillfully?"

"Why, I am embroidering this purse."

Chichikov is apparently dumbfounded; he opens his
mouth, but confused, he awkwardly leaves the room all the
while looking back at the design and at the genius who embroidered it.

"A pleasant man," the Governor decides and again returns
to his embroidery and his singing.

Stanislavski had turned what might easily have been an
insignificant, rather dull scene into one full of humor. In the
scene there is a beginning, a development and an end; the
Governor, who meets Chichikov with abhorrence, parts from
him as a friend; Chichikov, who had envisioned the Governor
a dragon, finds him, instead, a good-natured, silly creature
whom he can twist around his little finger. All the steps in the
development of the relationship between these two are clear-
cut, consistent, logical and gradual—and, therefore, convinc-

ing. However, it is one thing to think out and create the design of a scene but quite another to get from an actor a living, organic embodiment on the stage, to get a feeling that in the scene there are not actors but living people.

Stanislavski long ago began to understand that the chief secret of mastering a role lies in studying the physical behavior of the character. If this physical behavior is correct and interesting, then the speech pattern of the role will be naturally and easily formed. Angelina O. Stepanova, an outstanding artist of the Moscow Art Theatre, recalls her first work with Konstantin Sergeyevich. Although she was still a young actress, sixteen or seventeen years old, when she was accepted into the company of the Moscow Art Theatre, she was immediately given the role of the young Countess Mstislavskaya in *Tsar Fyodor* and called to rehearsal the same day. It was impossible to memorize the lines in such a short time; she came to the theatre, hid in a corner in fright and waited. When the rehearsal came to her scene, Stanislavski asked:

"Who is playing Mstislavskaya?"

The young actress came out shyly and was introduced to Konstantin Sergeyevich. He greeted her in a friendly way and asked her to go on the stage and rehearse.

"But I don't know anything. I haven't learned the lines."

"It's very good that you haven't learned them. Put down your notebook and go into the garden to meet your young man. He will climb over the fence. Wait for him . . . listen, try to guess where he will come from. Plan some kind of game; hide yourself, frighten him. You know how to do this. Well, now, begin."

"But what do I say?"

"Just say what you want to say in the given circumstances."

I remember similar episodes in my own experience. Several days before the season closed, I went to say good-bye to Konstantin Sergeyevich. It was at the height of our work on *Dead Souls.*

"How shall I work on the role during the vacation?" I asked.

"Don't take either the role or the play with you. Just rest, but in your leisure time put together plans for all kinds of swindles. Choose as your victim for these one or another of your neighbors and think carefully how you might become acquainted with him, how you could get into his confidence, how you might cheat him. Everything must be envisaged as if you seriously intended to carry it out in life. Having worked out one plan, start another against another neighbor who has a different character, income, position. This plan will be completely different from the first. Start each time with the question 'If I had to fool a man who has this or that quality, these characteristics, who is living in this or that place, etc.; if I had to rob him, let us say, how would I act under those circumstances?' On your return from your vacation, I'll expect you to tell me a number of entertaining stories about your clever 'thievery.' This will be of great use to you in mastering the character of Chichikov. I wish you success. Good-bye, have a good rest."

It was considered a virtue by some especially conscientious actors of the old school to come to the first rehearsal with a full knowledge of the text. This invariably delighted their directors, but it would have caused consternation to Konstantin Sergeyevich. He feared giving the actor the text too early. He saw the danger in the text "lying in the muscles of the tongue." The intonation of the dialogue should not be the result of the simple training of the muscles of the tongue. It would then necessarily be empty, cold and wooden, conveying nothing and set forever. This is bound to happen if the actor, without preparing the other complicated parts of his creative apparatus, begins work with the words of the author. On the other hand, the intonation will always be alive, organic and bright if it is the result of motivated, live images and clear ideas.

At one of the rehearsals of *Tartuffe*, Stanislavski said: "In the first place, it is necessary to set the logical sequence of your physical actions. In this way prepare the role. When the actor's work is built on the muscles of the tongue, it is mere hack work, but when the actor has images, *that* is creativity."

AT MANILOV'S

The scene with Manilov seemed to us very difficult and, in the beginning, even impossible to play. Its difficulty consists in the inability of our hero to determine his line of action. Everything that is written by Gogol is very interesting, bright and comprehensive, but how can one transfer this to the language of the stage, through what active channels can we express the inactivity of Manilov?

The future director M. N. Kedrov, who played the role of Manilov more believably than anyone else, found it impossible to create a design of the part without posing for himself definite, active tasks. However, to find these tasks was especially difficult. Kedrov could not answer the question: What does Manilov want? What does he passionately try to achieve in entertaining Paul Ivanovich Chichikov? The director Sakhnovsky proceeded along the line of discovering what kind of man Manilov was, but this could not satisfy that demanding actor Kedrov, who was trying to get the role on the right track. Sometimes Kedrov's arguments with the director dragged on and on and gave the impression of stubbornness or caprice.

"What don't you understand, Mikhail Nikolayevich?" asked Sakhnovsky.

"I don't understand anything."

"What do you mean, you don't understand anything? I simply don't know what else to tell you."

"Tell me what Manilov wants."

"Well, what *can* he want? You understand he is a cipher. He is a gap in humanity."

"That doesn't give me anything. How can he not want *anything?* This is what he says here: 'Paul Ivanovich, I beg you to sit down in this armchair. I reserve this chair especially for my guests.'"

"Well, what of it?"

"He wants him to sit in this special armchair for some reason."

"Oh, God! This is impossible, Mikhail Nikolayevich! For the most part, he is sentimental, you understand, and . . ."

"Yes, I know what kind of person he is, Gogol has told us. But here they are getting up from the table after dinner; Manilov begs Chichikov to eat some more, but Chichikov refuses and asks him to give him a little time for a business conversation. Manilov invites him into his study, places him in a comfortable armchair and offers him a pipe. In a long, dreamy monologue he drops a lot of compliments, pours out his joy at having Paul Ivanovich as his guest, dreams of a life with him 'in the shade of an elm tree,' and so on, and so on. Well, what is this? Everything is *in general: in general* he offers him food, *in general* he makes him sit down, *in general* he dreams. Where is the aim of all this hidden—where is his through-line-of-action? Only in dependence on the through-line-of-action can I decide how to do this. . . . What goal does Manilov have? For pity sakes, there *is* no objective here."

"But that cannot be, then there would be nothing to act; nobody will pay attention to that."

This kind of conversation occurred several times and was repeated endlessly in countless variations at every rehearsal. At that time I did not appreciate Kedrov's aspirations toward directing; he still could not explain his ideas with sufficient clarity. But in the end he was right. One must not play "in general." In the scene between Chichikov and Manilov there must be found a clear stage language, a language of action. Chichikov really has a definite and clear objective: to persuade Manilov to sell him dead souls. In order that the audience may see and follow the logic of his action, which is the most interesting thing, it is necessary that he overcome certain obstacles. These obstacles stem from the logic of the action of his partner, Manilov, but in order to recognize them, we must know what Manilov wants. It is, however, impossible to discover these desires in the abstract, without knowing what prompts them.

The task in this case was very difficult because of Manilov's character. If we simply begin to act everything just as it is written in the scene, Manilov may appear simply as a friendly, charming, even generous host, with whom Chichikov can very easily accomplish his business. But with Gogol's Manilov it seems this way only in the beginning, the further we go, the worse he becomes, and in a short time we begin to be sick of him. How can all this be shown on the stage? Through what *desires*, through what *actions*, shall we express it?

This is what Kedrov was trying to find in the rehearsals. There were attempts to get out of the impasse by playing some interesting outward characterizations and by using distorted intonations, but these were not successful.

Nevertheless, all the effort and investigations of Kedrov were not without results. From rehearsal to rehearsal, here and there, he made a number of successful discoveries. We began to feel that the scene might be brought off successfully, might be interesting. Some unique logic in the behavior of Manilov made itself felt and this was good. Kedrov was on the right track, but he lacked assurance; it was necessary for him to understand perfectly, to define by some accurate name, the logic of Manilov's behavior. So far he had been unable to do this; the feeling of insecurity did not leave him, and it was impossible not be aware of this.

The showing of the scene to Stanislavski began with something funny: when Kedrov and I had taken our places, Konstantin Sergeyevich, having said in his usual way: "Don't *play* anything, pretend I am not here," suggested that we begin. But as soon as we opened our mouths, he immediately turned to Sakhnovsky and started to whisper to him. We decided to wait, but Stanislavski's conversation with Sakhnovsky continued. We looked at each other and softly asked one another whether we should wait or start the scene. We even started to argue, until one of us insisted on starting. But as soon as we said the first line, we were stopped.

"What is it? Why do you suddenly overact? You started so well and then suddenly you *act.*"

"But we haven't started yet."

"Not started? Before you started to shout those lines, you accommodated yourselves to one another; you should continue in the same way. What is the meaning of this scene? Neither Manilov nor Chichikov wants to come into the room first. The scene is built on which of them can more cleverly defer to the other. You started very well. I was observing you all the time, in spite of the fact that I seemed busy in conversation, and suddenly you ruined everything . . . that's terrible!"

We didn't tell him what had really happened, and the rehearsal continued.

"Well, there is much here that is correct; you live truthfully," Konstantin Sergeyevich said at the end of the scene. "But do you feel what is needed here? This first purchase of dead souls is the most difficult, it is a touchstone. Chichikov has chosen Manilov for his first trial thinking that he would be a very easy subject, but it is necessary that he be the *most* difficult. How are we to do this? Where is the action and where is the counteraction? The task of Chichikov is clear, but it is necessary to give him obstacles. It is important that no matter what Manilov does, it should place Chichikov in the most difficult position for the accomplishment of his aim. So, Mikhail Nikolayevich, how will you seat Chichikov in the armchair? Try to place him in a very uncomfortable position; be moved by the beauty of it and then fall into despair if he attempts to change it. And you, Vasily Osipovich, try to change your position unnoticeably and get ready for an intimate conversation. You, Mikhail Nikolayevich, follow this closely and don't give him the chance to change the pose; on the contrary, make it even more intricate. In this there is already an element of conflict; look for it."

We performed several exercises under the observation of Konstantin Sergeyevich.

"Do you realize the difference between the tasks of Manilov and Chichikov? If Manilov were simply a cordial, hospitable, generous host, the task would be simpler. The efforts of such a host give pleasure to his guest; but this is not the case here. Manilov gives pleasure to himself and tortures his guest. He is really only interested in setting up attractive groupings. All his concerns about his guest are the concerns of a photographer trying to place a group for a picture:

" 'Here I am having dinner with Paul Ivanovich. Here we are sitting in armchairs philosophizing. Here I, my wife and Paul Ivanovich are dreaming of life under the same roof, etc.'

"Do you see how this might exhaust one's patience? And especially that of Chichikov, who came to talk about a very delicate business.

"Try to do something of that kind here."

The task pleased us. Here was something to get hold of, and we took to the work. Developing the theme given by Stanislavski, we were more and more fascinated by the etude and found a whole series of very bright, humorous moments; but, most important, we felt support, we understood where the clash, the fight, the conflict lay.

"Is it clear to you what the essence of this scene is? Chichikov, who has come on very complicated and dangerous business, stumbles on a man who uses the arrival of Paul Ivanovich as an excuse to make a whole series of 'photographs' on the theme: 'The Arrival of Paul Ivanovich at My Estate.' Do you understand how different their tasks are and how each prevents the other from achieving his goal? How difficult it is for Chichikov to overcome the 'photographer' obsessed with his own fantastically sentimental photographs and bring him down to earth; but, on the other hand, how difficult Manilov's task will be to incorporate into his photographs the unexpectedly emerging dead souls!

"Each puts maximum temperament into his action. Chichikov can hardly control his fury, but is obliged to be polite and tactful and to find some clever trick in order, finally, to take the initiative into his own hands. And later, when the strange request has been made and Manilov stands speechless, wondering whether he is dealing with a madman, how much effort, how much cleverness is necessary on Chichikov's part to bring Manilov to his senses and assure him that this transaction with dead souls will finally strengthen their unusual bonds of friendship. Believing this, Manilov, inflamed with enthusiasm, undertakes to create an idealistic group, in which both his wife and children will take part. Here the most difficult task for Chichikov is to tear himself away from Manilov's house by any means; the task of Manilov is, even at the expense of his life, not to let him out. Do you feel the rhythm of this? You are playing the scene languidly but it should be filled with passion. Try the beginning of the scene. Chichikov gets up from the table with a full stomach, but the Manilovs want to force him to eat more. They do not just *offer* food, I mean exactly what I said—'force.' They force, demand, insist, and you, Chichikov, must cleverly evade them. You create a whole scene out of this; then a similar conflict follows at the door about who will go into the study first. Chichikov will leave Manilov wet with perspiration. Do you understand all this?"

"Yes, certainly."

"Well, then, try to *do* it; but until you can, don't consider that you have understood it."

Obviously, a good deal of work was still to be done, but the delightful concreteness of Stanislavski's instructions cleared the way for us to overcome the difficult material and encouraged us to think it possible to embody Gogol's characters sharply and clearly.

At Nozdrov's

Working on the production of *Dead Souls*, Stanislavski quite often held meetings with the directors, talked with them and criticized their work. After one of these meetings, we asked Sakhnovsky to tell us what they had talked about. Vasily Grigorovich told us that there had been, in the first place, some critical remarks about the actors and the direction the production was taking, its weak spots and possible means of strengthening them. (Each criticism of Stanislavski's was worked out subsequently by the actors.)

"No mise en scène is needed," Stanislavski said, "just a background which permits me to see the eyes of the actors without distracting me. They are sitting opposite each other and talking; I am interested only in the life in their eyes."

In the search for this suitable background, Konstantin Sergeyevich rejected two designs submitted by V. V. Dmitriev and, although not completely satisfied with it, approved the third by Simov only as a compromise. After rejecting Dmitriev's first design, Konstantin Sergeyevich suggested the following: In the playing area, that is, in that place where the scene develops (and this place must always be limited), everything should be quite finished and executed with reality and completeness; but the further from the center, the more the set should take on a diffused form, having the look of a charcoal sketch. In the model the set looked quite interesting, but when the sets were put on the stage and the actors appeared, it was evident that such a set would distract attention. The mounting of the play was then given to Simov who proposed a system of neutral draperies which limited the set to the playing area. This was followed in the performance.

In the conversation with Sakhnovsky, Konstantin Sergeyevich had spoken repeatedly about how to work with actors.

"You, Vasily Grigorovich, have the ability to 'show' the actor. You have acting talent, undoubtedly. You should try to act. But showing the actor seldom achieves the objective. It is important to be able to offer him enticements. The art of the director-teacher consists of this. There are actors who possess a vivid imagination which you only have to start in the right direction; there are others whose imagination has to be awakened again and again, to whom you have to offer something constantly for them to develop. You must not confuse these two types of actors; you cannot apply the same method to both. You must not give the actor anything ready-made. Let him come to what you want by himself. Your business is to help him by placing in his way some enticing excitement. But you must know under what circumstances you must entice."

Vasily Grigorovich tried not to leave out anything which had been said by Konstantin Sergeyevich and concluded in this way:

"Well, it seems I have told you everything. Now forget it. Konstantin Sergeyevich earnestly requested that we keep silent about this and not discuss anything."

This remarkable ability of Stanislavski to entice the actor, to stimulate his imagination and creative activity, enabled him at times to create moments of great inspiration, even in rehearsal. I remember some of the rehearsals of the scenes between Chichikov and Nozdrov; bright, temperamental scenes between these two swindlers. Here was Chichikov's first failure; one that had a disastrous result for him.

I. M. Moskvin played with unusual humor and temperament and this scene somehow went better than the others for me. Even before our meeting with Stanislavski, this scene was very good to watch, so we were eager to show it, hoping for his complete approval. But the showing had to be delayed because of trifles. The whole scene went well and with considerable tautness until the game of checkers. During the game, the two players taunt each other with the usual jibes: "I haven't had checkers in my hands for a long time," says one.

"Everyone knows how badly you play," answers the other.

This game spoiled everything for us. It suddenly stopped the scene which had been running so well. We couldn't discover what we had to do so that the game would not interrupt the flow of the scene. Nozdrov is really trying to make Chichikov drunk in order to involve him in a questionable deal. Chichikov refuses the drink so as to keep his head clear so he can complete *his* swindle with the dead souls. Nozdrov, feeling that his guest has some kind of offer to make him, sends his brother-in-law out of the room and remains face to face with Chichikov. These two thieves then begin to try to trap each other. The moment Nozdrov hears Chichikov's wish to buy the "dead ones," he overwhelms him with suggestions. At first he offers them as a present, but with the consideration that Chichikov buy his stallion very cheap, or his mare or his dog, or at least the puppy; he offers them in exchange for a carriage, or he offers to gamble at cards for them. Chichikov refuses all these offers, thereby enraging Nozdrov. Chichikov, finally offended by the insults thrown at him, tries to slip out of Nozdrov's grasp and get away from his estate, but to no avail. The incensed, reckless gambler Nozdrov will not let his victim go so easily. He offers to play a game of checkers:

"This is not like cards, where everything is sharp practice and fraud; here everything depends upon skill."

Chichikov is tempted because he knows his mastery of this game and sits down to play, placing a hundred rubles against all of Nozdrov's dead souls.

Until this moment, the scene, as I said before, went well; without any particular finesse, perhaps, but with a certain excitement, temperament and good humor. But as soon as we had settled down to play, the energy stopped. The ending became weak and destroyed all our previous work.

What we didn't try! Shortening the scene by speeding up the tempo, cutting, coloring separate moments in the game by using funny tricks, employing a variety of intonations, making up our own words, and, finally, cutting the game of checkers completely. But nothing satisfied us. Difficulty with this section forced us to delay showing it to Stanislavski. We wanted to find the solution ourselves and then show him the scene in all its brilliance. Unfortunately, we never succeeded in doing this, and we went to the demonstration with it as it was; maybe somehow we would succeed.

"Well, what do you yourselves think of this? Did you succeed with this scene or not?" Stanislavski asked after the showing. "What do you consider successful and what not successful in your presentation?"

"Is it possible to cut the game of checkers?"

"Why?"

"Because it spoils the whole thing. We tried it every way, but nothing worked. It is difficult to play. It somehow comes out superfluous—useless."

"But that is the most remarkable part of the whole scene— playing checkers. Doesn't it seem so to you?"

"It stops the rhythm of the scene."

"Indeed! At the moment of greatest tension in the scene, suddenly there is violent rhythm."

"We don't understand. They just sit there and move the checkers."

"Have you never been to a chess tournament? There they also just sit and move the chessmen, but all the while there are exceptionally tense moments. You say that you worked very hard on this scene. That's good, but evidently the work didn't go in the right direction. Tell me how you worked, what you did."

We told him in detail.

"Hm! . . . Hm! . . ." A pause. "What stakes did Chichikov have in this game?"

"A hundred rubles."

"And Nozdrov?"

"Nozdrov . . . he . . . he didn't place anything, he played for the dead souls."

"So." A pause. "And how many does he have?"

"How many what?"

"Dead ones."

Silence.

"I asked you how many dead souls Nozdrov had?"

"Well . . . approximately . . . It was not said how many. Probably, quite a lot. We don't know."

"What do you mean, 'don't know?' And you, Vasily Osipovich, *you* don't know?" he said to me.

"Absolutely not."

"Good gracious! Why not? It means you . . . what did I teach you!? Hm! . . . Hm! . . . We are going in completely opposite directions. Ah! Ah! Ah! We must start from the beginning! Naturally, you could not play this scene, no matter how much you struggled with it. You do not know the chief reason for your game—how large the stake is! It is one thing when a person plays for five kopeks, but quite another thing when it is for one's whole fortune. That is a completely different matter. Before you begin to work, you must know first what you want to do. What title would you give this scene? 'The Play of Fools,' 'Reckless Play,' or 'Life or Death' or something else? You are trying to do something without knowing what. Naturally, your work didn't succeed. You were searching for ornaments, tricks, not for the essence. Well, how many dead souls could Nozdrov have?"

We spent the rest of the rehearsal in lively conversation about the landowner's life, about his serfs. We reread parts of *Dead Souls*. We had to fix the position of Nozdrov among the landowners; we speculated about how much he was worth and tried to calculate how many dead souls he might have at that moment. Konstantin Sergeyevich led the conversation, cleverly directing it into the right channel, not letting it deviate from the question at hand.

Finally it was determined: Nozdrov might have up to two hundred dead serfs who were still counted alive, the ones whom Chichikov could buy. If he won and mortgaged them to the Guardian Council for two hundred rubles apiece, he would receive forty thousand in cash.

"Do you understand now what kind of game Chichikov is playing? Risking a hundred rubles, he may win forty thousand. That is a considerable fortune. This is what you have to understand completely. From the start you should feel how important each move in the game is, what Chichikov lives through when this extremely large sum is lost because of Nozdrov's cheating. Think about everything and try to understand what you would do in the given circumstances."

With this, Stanislavski dismissed us. The next meeting, which took place very soon afterward, was devoted exclusively to the game of checkers. Konstantin Sergeyevich questioned me minutely. He asked if I played cards or gambled on a large scale; whether I won or lost a lot, how this happened; how I acted in real life at the pitch of excitement, etc. I told him some episodes out of my past.

"Then try to realize from that what the inner rhythm of the gambler is at the decisive moment of playing. Can you tell me how he acts?

"He has to win at all costs. Perhaps there is a question of honor, of life—whatever you like. Checkers—this is not a game of luck, but of knowledge or calculation. In order not to miss, not to lose the opportune moment for a successful combination, how must you mobilize yourself? Recall those moments about which you spoke so interestingly. Like the time you risked a large sum in Irkutsk."

"I felt then that . . ."

"No. I don't want your feelings, tell me how you behaved. Now, recall . . ."

"I watched how the banker looked at his hand and tried to guess what high cards he had and what I should do—buy more or stop on five?"

"And he?"

"He, it seemed to me, watched me very attentively too."

"Why do you think *attentively?*"

"I saw this from his eyes."

"What color are Moskvin's eyes? Why are you checking now? You should know that already. You played checkers with him many times in rehearsal! You *really* don't remember the color of his eyes? Surely you recall the eyes of your Irkutsk partner? What is missing in you now? What do you lack? How did you lose the excitement of the game this time? You were not attentive to your partner Moskvin. You completely missed the element of attention, *sharp* attention. You should have begun your work with this: train your attention, give it tasks, be attentive to the actions of your partner, at first to his more obvious actions, later, to the more subtle ones. If, after acting a certain scene, you sharply recall all the barely perceptible subtleties of the action of your partner, it means that you yourself played the scene well; you had the most important stage quality—concentration. When you played cards in Irkutsk, you did this instinctively, being aware of the catastrophe which threatened you if you should lose. On the stage there is no *real* danger, nevertheless you should know from experience how you must act. Train yourself in these actions. Do you know how to play checkers well?"

"No, quite badly."

"Put the checkers on the board; begin to play. . . . Why did you make that move? Before making it, think two or three moves ahead and try to anticipate how Moskvin may respond and in what position your checkers will be afterward. Concentrate all your attention on this. . . . Did you guess Moskvin's moves?"

"No."

"Go on playing, only plan two moves ahead; meanwhile, watch Moskvin's left hand—he will try to take your hundred rubles from the table. Ivan Mikhailovich, try to do that. You, Vasily Osipovich, cover the bills before Ivan Mikhailovich moves his hand even a little bit in their direction. Think, think of your moves. Now then, continue to play. Only play naturally and to the end of the game. We shall see which of you plays better. . . . Eh! You see, your hundred rubles have disappeared. This is because of your inattention. Attention, attention and *more* attention. Ivan Mikhailovich, you cheated too noticeably; Chichikov will immediately refuse to play with you. It is necessary to find the exact moment for this. Continue to play."

These exercises continued for a long time. Finally, that transformation occurred which comes as a result of knowing the true direction and consistency of a work. We had become seriously involved in our game; we followed each other's movements attentively and, as a result, the rhythm of our sitting became appropriately restless. Now we felt the strained attention of two reckless gamblers. Our agitated inner rhythm was in contrast to the outward quiet we assumed in speaking our lines. Thus the real embodiment of the two characters was underlined. I saw how Moskvin's eyes sparkled. Eventually this became our favorite scene in the whole play.

Even much later, after *Dead Souls* had opened and was placed in the repertory, the further perfecting of it was the continuing care of the directors and of Stanislavski himself.

Not even a replacement in a secondary part, not to mention the leading roles, could be introduced into the production without the review and approval of Stanislavski.

The role of Nozdrov was sometimes played by V. N. Livanov, a very talented character actor with indefatigable imagination and an exuberant temperament for comedy. He was a wonderful caricaturist, but his impatience, his desire to "catch" the character quickly always created some chaos in the first stages of work. His playing then seemed confused, often superficial. Being a talented person, he couldn't help recognizing this himself, but he suffered through his temporary failures until he finally found the correct embodiment of the character. Such was the case with the role of Nozdrov. The role was completely within his ability and he liked it, but not being satisfied with the text or the staging, he added to his part much that was new and different from what was in Gogol's poem. He put in a whole monologue about how joyful Nozdrov had felt at a fair where he had made merry with some officers, especially a certain Lieutenant Kuvshinikov, with whom Nozdrov was sure Chichikov would also have made friends. We showed this scene to Stanislavski. In rehearsal, Livanov didn't play this scene badly, but all the same he could have played it better. In his acting the real inner gaiety, the infectiousness of Nozdrov, was missing; it followed only the line of outward expression. The monologue was very difficult, demanding a high quality of acting with considerable technique.

"Now then, my dear fellow . . . all this is correct . . . more or less . . . but a little inaccurate. You are not communicating, you are not seeing. Are you telling us what you really did with those officers at the fair?"

Livanov, a man, as I have said, with a great imagination, played a number of variations on what might have taken place in the company of drunken officers. Stanislavski listened to him a little absentmindedly, as if contemplating something, and finally said:

"All that is just child's play. Were they *real* officers?"

And then he told us things that made us drop our jaws in surprise; for a long time we could not collect ourselves. We fell into uncontrollable laughter, which we suppressed with difficulty in order to listen further to what Stanislavski was saying. He was inspired. He drew for us picture after picture of the revelry, the scandal of the officers' behavior at the fair, each brighter and more colorful than the last. When he told us in detail exactly what Lieutenant Kuvshinikov had done that had made such an impression on Nozdrov, we fell off our chairs. How such images could arise in the mind of such a modest, innocent person as Stanislavski was a mystery that gave special sharpness to his narrative.

When, after quieting down, we began to repeat the scene,

Nozdrov's monologue sounded altogether different. Livanov's eyes sparkled, they shone. Before his inner vision passed the bright images of Stanislavski; he was *very* aware of them. He expended all his energy in the search for a variety of colors to communicate to Chichikov his vivid impressions of the officers' orgy. When the image of Lieutenant Kuvshinikov drawn by Stanislavski came to the surface of Livanov's imagination, he could hardly pronounce the word "Lieutenant" before such a spasm of laughter gripped him that he could only give vent to his feelings and laugh to his heart's content. The laughter was alive, it was human laughter, seizing all his being. This was the infectious laughter of Nozdrov. This was Gogol.

In general the rehearsal was gay and joyous. Konstantin Sergeyevich was in a good mood, to which Livanov, himself a very witty person, contributed not a little, always alternating the work and conversation with amusing jokes. So, when we had successfully completed this scene, Konstantin Sergeyevich turned to him with the words:

"My good fellow, this is now simply marvelous, it is a masterpiece."

"Well, yes," answered Livanov, "but one can't repeat it a second time."

"By no means."

"That's the trouble. You say it is a masterpiece, but what is the good of it? If, let us say, it were a painting I might have sold it at once, but all we have is . . . *fou-fou.*"

Konstantin Sergeyevich laughed for a long time and in saying good-bye to Livanov tried to quiet his protestations, saying that our art has its advantages too. But Livanov, carrying on his joke, merely brushed him aside and continued to bewail his lost masterpiece.

One day at one of the rehearsals of *Dead Souls* in Stanislavski's study in Leontyev Lane, the talk turned to new directions in theatre art. Konstantin Sergeyevich, because of his illness at this time, no longer visited the theatres. Therefore he listened to our reports of the Moscow performances with interest and attention. We told him about the contrivances of the "formalistic" directors, who at that time were much respected by some theatre groups, the "modern" ones especially, who considered that they represented advanced art which might bring about a change from the "decrepit, academic" Moscow Art Theatre.

"We must regard this calmly and courageously," said Konstantin Sergeyevich. "We must continue to perfect our art, our technique. There are false searchings and directions in art which at the time seem the last word. They threaten the foundations of high realistic art, but they are unable to destroy it completely. Formalism is a temporary phase. One must just wait till it is over; not sitting with hands folded, but working. Someone must take care to preserve the living sprouts of our genuine, great art which are now being choked by the weeds. One can rest assured that the weeds will perish and the time will come when the sprouts will have attained their full growth and blossom magnificently. But it is necessary to nourish the sprouts. This difficult task lies with us. This is our sacred responsibility, our debt to art."

His words were cheerful and confidence and light shone in his eyes. But later, listening to an account of a performance of Shakespeare's *Hamlet* in one of the Moscow theatres, where, at the whim of the director, the marvelous character of the thinker-philosopher was performed in a comic manner, and the poetic Ophelia was converted into a profligate woman, Stanislavski at once drooped and, taking a deep breath, said sadly:

"Ah. . . . There art is ruined."

Then, energetically, he began to work. That day he was especially critical of us, attacking the smallest blunder or show of bad taste. He was sometimes cruel and unjust. We were paying for those who had outraged the genius of Shakespeare.

AT PLUSHKIN'S

The marvelous chapter in Gogol's *Dead Souls* about Plushkin lends itself rather poorly to dramatization. Plushkin is sitting in his room. Chichikov comes in and, having taken him for the housekeeper, enters into conversation with him. Later, after discovering his mistake, Chichikov masks his scheme under the guise of charity to the unfortunate old man. Wheedling out of Plushkin his agreement to sell his dead souls, Chichikov leaves the estate of the stingy landowner. The wonderful artist Leonidov, who played Plushkin, had all the gifts needed for the embodiment of this character. Leonidov's age, the keenness and individuality of his interesting personality, his piercing, suspicious glance, his voice—strong, but with the timbre of a tenor, a voice which at times seemed almost womanly—his natural inclination toward tragedy, all this assured us that the role of Plushkin was in competent hands. Leonidov would be able to show the deep, tragic aspect of a man, once an excellent master and family man, an outstanding Russian landowner, now consumed by a fatal passion. But how can an actor reveal all the complicated features of the character so minutely, lovingly and richly described in the poem? No dramatization can encompass the remarkable descriptions and poetic digressions of Gogol; in the dramatization there was only a business conversation about the sale of dead souls, and that was all.

This got on Leonidov's nerves. He felt that there was not enough time to develop the role's possibilities and to display his own temperament.

Leonidov treated Stanislavski with great respect and each rehearsal with Konstantin Sergeyevich was for him an exciting event. He did not wish to present himself insufficiently prepared at the first demonstration for Stanislavski, so he worked strenuously and was overdemanding of himself and of me, his partner. My role went badly and he tried to help me in every way, understanding perfectly well that the lack of a good Chichikov could once and for all ruin his part.

Although the miserly Plushkin was convincingly expressed by Leonidov, the scene was only interesting in spots and in general did not hold the audience's attention. A small audience was always present at our rehearsals; if we could not succeed in capturing it, then what could we expect from the unknown audience which would fill the auditorium on the day of the performance? But this was far in the future; our immediate concern was showing our work to Stanislavski.

I had never before seen Konstantin Sergeyevich in such deep concentration at a rehearsal as on that day when we played the Plushkin scene for him for the first time. His attention was directed not toward me, but toward Leonidov.

I played weakly, felt my helplessness, but Stanislavski completely ignored me; I did not exist for him. He followed the acting of Leonidov, watching him intently as if he feared to miss his smallest movement, breath, inflection. Stanislavski didn't move, but his thoughts showed on his face, at which, I confess, I looked once in a while. His expression most of the time was not favorable.

We finished. Then came a long, tormenting pause.

Taking off his pince-nez and staring into space, Stanislavski seemed to be searching for words for his sad diagnosis.

Leonidov, pale, waited with downcast eyes.

I, because of my hopelessness, pretended complete indifference and calm. The director and the assistants prepared to take notes.

"Hm! . . . Hm! . . . Very good. You, Leonid Mironovich, have found much that is good." A long pause. "But all this is somewhat without form—all this is 'in general.' There is no design, and your colors, although good, do not work. In the scene there is no beginning, no development, no climax and no end. You must search out where Plushkin is good . . . not good, but generous—where he is a spendthrift, a debauchee, and you must make this the top of the role. Then your stinginess will show; it will be especially sharp and powerful in the final scene when he says: 'No, I will leave him the watch in my will so that he will remember me.' Through what can you express his stinginess? Only through the events which happen to him, but you give him very little attention. You keep going deeper and deeper into yourself, into your own inner world, but throughout the whole scene you are afraid to show the feelings of a miser, and that is not right. You must start from what happens to Plushkin. Play each moment to the full in all its details. Only this path will lead you to the development of the character.

"What happened? Plushkin returned home after his usual search for rubbish, with a basket of trash, which he added to the heap already lying on the floor of his room. But for Plushkin this was not rubbish, not trash, this was a rich collection of rare antiques.

"He had been absent for a long time; the house had been empty and he was certain there were bandits in the neighborhood. How difficult it had been to avoid being robbed as he made his way home with his basket of treasures! Coming into the room, he took in the premises at a glance, in order to make sure that in his absence nobody had interfered with his household.

"Having relaxed a little, he settled himself beside the pile and began to pick up and count the objects in his collection. At this moment the curtain opens and your scene begins.

"Here is the beginning of the action. The audience sees Plushkin and his room for the first time. Everything there is interesting. You do not need to hurry. You may play a big scene here: 'Plushkin Surveys His Treasures.' Can you play that? Only that?

"Do you realize what wonderful material this is for an actor? If you play this scene in all its details, with its whole organic quality, without uttering a single word you can hold the audience's attention completely. But you lose this opportunity, you ignore it and hurry on quickly to the dialogue with Chichikov.

"You think that your salvation is there, but that is not true. Before Chichikov has spoken his first line, how many events have taken place, how many emotional experiences? All this is very interesting to us and to the audience. Here we see how an old man, looking like an old woman, digs into a pile of trash with great attention and lovingly inspects each piece which he takes out, whether it is a horseshoe or a piece of the sole of an old shoe. He is so deeply absorbed that he does not notice when the door is carefully opened and Chichikov appears in the room. Chichikov begins to observe Plushkin attentively, trying to distinguish if this is a woman or a man. Feeling his gaze, Plushkin turns to Chichikov and their glances meet.

"What does this mean for Plushkin? This is what he most fears, what has been his continual nightmare: that a bandit might sneak into his treasure house. And what a bandit! Not one of those who live here, near his estate—he knows all those—no, this is a new one, a newcomer obviously, probably a specialist in robbery and murder.

"What to do? After the first moment of shock, Plushkin begins to take precautions for saving his life. He carefully hides his fear of the bandit in order to try to sneak out of the room and call for help.

"Under these circumstances it is very difficult for Chichikov to start a conversation. This is a very interesting moment in their mutual misunderstanding, in their striving for two opposite goals—one, to start a conversation and the other, to flee from the room.

"Finally, the first words are spoken, the positions become more or less clear, and the dialogue begins.

"But you begin with the dialogue right away, leaving out the most interesting moment—the moment of orientation, the moment they become acquainted with each other.

"In life you never leave this out, but on the stage, for some reason, you do.

"I assure you, this is very important; this most of all convinces the audience. The actor's belief in his own action places him on the path of truth. This is most important.

"The moment of orientation may be short, hardly perceptible; it depends on the circumstances. The moment of orientation, the feeling out of each other, does not end invariably when the partners enter into conversation. Their first words usually do not sound really effective because each has not made for himself even a preliminary evaluation of his partner. They continue to feel each other out in order to have greater influence on one another. This is especially true with such a suspicious person as Plushkin.

"You see, before he finds out who this Chichikov is, before he comes to believe that Chichikov is none other than a messenger from heaven who is bringing him a blessing in reward for his great good nature and humility, he had taken him for a robber, then for a landowner who had come as a guest expecting to dine well, then for a ruined hussar who wished to borrow money, etc. Here, each time, are moments of orientation with appropriate patterns of behavior followed by changes of orientation and new patterns in conformity with the new circumstances which arise.

"This first part of the scene is like a prelude: 'Plushkin Recognizes Chichikov.' For now, this is all you must do; forget everything else, just play these moments of orientation with attention and note your impressions.

"The second part is 'Plushkin Finally Understands That a Benefactor Is Before Him.' How can he show him kindness, gain his favor and keep it? This is where Plushkin arranges a 'banquet.' He orders the servant to bring in the samovar and some dried crumbs of kulich [Easter cake], which his relatives had brought him three years ago. This is a rich landowner, a hospitable person, giving an unprecedented banquet! Play Plushkin here as a generous spendthrift; forget completely about his stinginess and give yourself one task—to feast your benefactor, to astonish him with your generosity while at the same time quickly advancing the business of selling the dead souls.

"During the second part of this scene there are two crucial moments when the transaction almost fails: one, because Plushkin is not able to go into town, the other, because he cannot find a piece of clean paper on which to write the agreement.

"These moments are very serious; do not let them pass, play each one to the end.

"The loss of the piece of paper is for Plushkin a big event. Here it is most important to search for the paper truthfully. Only in this way can you transmit the complete depth of your emotional experience. Great concentration, genuine attention are necessary. In short, don't play emotion, *act*.

"Finally, these obstacles are overcome and the business completed: not only dead but runaway souls are bought by this astonishing benefactor, Paul Ivanovich Chichikov.

"Now, the third part of the scene: Plushkin considers how best to behave toward this exceptional person who has done him so much good. What's more, he even refused refreshment.

"Think of only one thing—how to express your love, your respect, your gratitude to your guest. Forget completely about Plushkin, the gloomy, bitter grumbler, the misanthrope.

"No, suddenly he is especially amiable, a philanthropist.

"Here is the concluding part of the scene: 'Plushkin Remains Alone.' For a moment after Chichikov has left, Plushkin is concerned about whether he has requited his kind guest sufficiently. Suddenly it occurs to him that he has expressed his gratitude to this man badly. He hurries to the window where he sees Chichikov just getting into his carriage. Plushkin runs first to the heap of rubbish, then to his desk, fighting his desire to compensate for his omission.

"Finally, his lofty feelings triumph and the decision is made; he fussily digs into the dusty drawers of the desk saying:

'I will give him a pocket watch.' The watch is found. 'He is still a young man, he needs a watch in order to impress his fiancée . . . etc.' He blows the dust from the watch and, looking at it thoughtfully, runs to the door. But halfway there, he stops.

"This is what is called a 'pause for effect.' Here we see a man who, a moment earlier, had been burning with the desire to give a gift, horrified at the realization of the ruin into which his unpardonable extravagance has nearly brought him.

"This thought does not come to him at once. The moment of its conception and development must be expressed in the pause. When he understands all the implications, the task which arises before him is how he may hide that 'jewel' which nearly slipped away from him. He cannot rest until he makes sure that it is securely hidden, that he has found the safest place to store it.

"Finally this task is accomplished, but what of his benefactor? No matter, 'I will leave it to him in my will so that he will remember me.'

"Thus Plushkin again becomes Plushkin. He begins to examine his belongings with concern: has his unexpected visitor made off with something?

"At this the curtain falls.

"Each of these sections must be truthful; each must be played in logical sequence; all the actions must develop and unite what has been built up previously in an uninterrupted line of action.

"Don't think of the character, of the emotional experience. You just have a series of episodes, each different. Don't paint everything in one color of stinginess or gloominess. There is also kindness, generosity and joy here. Accordingly, Plushkin's actions are varied. In his unexpected change from one action to another, often completely opposite ones, the behavior of a miser in such matters is revealed. Expand each episode to the full; create events out of everything. Develop, above all, the scheme of your physical behavior in each episode and unite them later in a single line of action. This is the infallible way to bring about the embodiment of Gogol's Plushkin."

"And what should be my line of action, Konstantin Sergeyevich?" I asked.

"In every instance you must be able to adjust yourself to the character of your partner. Plushkin *is* a difficult case, but you have to get to the core of him. You, Chichikov, must be able to please Plushkin. How? Put yourself in Plushkin's place and consider what he wants. Everybody thinks of him as a miser, but you are surprised at his generosity, his hospitality. But you must do this in a way that will make him believe you. This is what Plushkin says about his neighbor, the captain: 'He is a relative,' he says, 'an uncle, an *uncle,* but he kisses my hand.' Do you see? Plushkin does not believe the captain although he kisses his hand; therefore it is necessary to act more subtly.

"You have to be sincerely filled with all the troubles of Plushkin; you must understand them and sympathize with him. You must become Plushkin at this time.

"Perhaps it would be good for a time for you to rehearse not Chichikov but Plushkin and the other landowners with whom he has to deal; unquestionably this will be of help to you."

The second player of the role of Plushkin was B. Y. Petker, who came to the Moscow Art Theatre, as I had, from the Moscow Theatre of Comedy, formerly the Korsh. This young actor played character roles very successfully and when the need arose for an understudy for Leonidov in the role of Plushkin, the choice fell on him. In this way Konstantin Sergeyevich became acquainted with our new artist through practical work.

After Petker had had several rehearsals of the play with E. S. Telesheva and Sakhnovsky, rehearsals were arranged with Stanislavski.

Petker was called one or two hours earlier than the rest of us; what happened in my absence was told me by Petker himself.

At the appointed time, Petker entered the little courtyard where Stanislavski sat at a table under a great linen umbrella. Near him were seated the directors Telesheva and Sakhnovsky. At some distance sat the artist Simov and the Turkish director Miskhy-Bey, lately come to Moscow for a theatre festival, who was interested in questions of directing technique and had received permission from Stanislavski to be present at the rehearsal.

Stanislavski greeted Petker very warmly, presenting him to Simov and Miskhy-Bey.

After a pause, Konstantin Sergeyevich asked the directors how the rehearsals were going, what was succeeding or not succeeding in the work.

After receiving reassuring answers to a series of questions, he asked:

"And how about Petker's age? You know Plushkin is at least seventy years old. This is a very difficult problem."

But the directors tried to reassure him.

"Boris Yakovlevich played very well," they said. "He has played many old men and is accustomed to it."

"Hm! . . . Hm! . . . I am very much afraid that this might be 'acting like' an old man. Look at any young man and see how well he plays an old one—he is often inadequate. He would not be at all interesting playing this character with the clichés of stinginess. Well, let's try it. Begin any place in the scene. Vasily Grigorovich, prompt me. I will play Chichikov. So, let us begin."

Petker, within the limits of his capacity, attempted to portray a decrepit, stingy old man by the usual formula.

Konstantin Sergeyevich, giving the cues, attentively followed him; then he stopped and put the question:

"With whom are you conversing? Who is sitting in front of you?"

"Konstantin Sergeyevich Stanislavski."

"Nothing of the kind—a swindler."

"How is that?"

"There! You see, you are already looking at me more attentively than when you played the scene. Now there is something alive. If I were a known swindler, how would you look at me during a conversation? Simply look at me as at a swindler. Try to divine my intentions, to define them. Suddenly you think, 'Does he have a hidden knife?' Imagine you have laid something down, something whose loss you fear. Don't play anything, just visualize it for yourself. You still want to *play* something, but you will not be able to really play anything until you have built up images."

Then Konstantin Sergeyevich reached for his pen, which was lying on the table, in order to take notes, but Petker, with a quick movement, grabbed it.

"Perfectly true. Now try to guess what else I want to do. Watch me. No, don't act, really watch. Ah! Again he *acts!* Let us take a walk. I am your neighbor and this is your estate. Tell me in detail how things are going with you. What's this barn for?" he asked seriously, pointing to a building.

Petker answered with some kind of general remarks, but Konstantin Sergeyevich was not satisfied with them and made even more detailed inquiries about many small things.

At that time a carter with a load of goods came into the courtyard. Konstantin Sergeyevich at once made his way to him, asking Petker on the way what this man was bringing and for whom.

Petker gave an explanation. Stanislavski listened attentively but repeated his question until he had received a satisfactory answer. So they walked about the courtyard and in a very serious tone continued their playing; then they sat down at the table and went on with their conversation about household themes: the mowing, the harvest, the peasants, etc.

At that point, I came into the rehearsal. Seeing Konstantin Sergeyevich engaged in serious conversation with Petker and not at all thinking that they were rehearsing, I stopped at a distance, waiting for a moment when it would be appropriate to greet them.

Konstantin Sergeyevich, stealing a glance at me, quietly whispered to Petker:

"Look who came in. Be very cautious with him, don't let him come nearer—he is a swindler."

I understood at once what was going on and joined in the playing.

Stanislavski, having created with us a field of action, quickly changed from landowner to director and began to observe us attentively.

I walked toward Petker but he quickly jumped up and ran away.

"Hm! . . . Hm! . . . You were acting, Boris Yakovlevich. You must just move away several steps, that is all. Now, approach him again, Vasily Osipovich. Hm! . . . Again, you are *acting!* . . . If you do it that way, Chichikov will realize at once that you are afraid of him. Do only what is necessary in order to be out of danger."

Petker and I began to talk, at the beginning improvising our own words, later turning to the author's text. Each time our conversation became theatrical acting and lost its organic flow, Konstantin Sergeyevich interrupted and again and again brought us back to the truth.

"You don't have to *play* anything, Petker, you need only listen and try to figure out what Chichikov is aiming at. All that is necessary is for you to make me aware of the focus of your attention. Try to guess why this unbidden guest has come. Now invite him to sit down. . . . No, you cannot do it that way; he will thrust a knife at you. . . . And that is not good either . . . find a more comfortable way . . . one less dangerous."

Step by step Stanislavski aroused real feelings in Petker and eliminated everything mediocre and theatrical. His cliché of senility vanished and a living face appeared with attentive, distrustful eyes. I responded to this and we both began to sense the thread of mutual interest binding us to each other.

I began guardedly to state my business. He listened to me, tried to grasp the heart of the matter.

We felt good. Our small audience was caught up in our conversation and paid attention to its development.

The moment came when Petker/Plushkin fully understood and appreciated the "good deed" which Chichikov wanted to do for him. After Chichikov's line "Out of respect for you I will take the expense of the purchase upon myself," his face brightened. For a long time he looked at me with amazement. Our audience waited with interest for further developments. Petker's face twitched convulsively. Konstantin Sergeyevich, who up to this time had been sitting in silence trying not to interrupt the scene which was now on the right track, carefully prompted:

"Now, *over*act; overact with your face, overact as much as you like. Now you have the right to do this. Wrinkle your face as much as you can, stick out your tongue ... more ... more ... Don't be afraid now. ... That's right!"

He laughed joyfully as he spoke and everyone around laughed too. With this, Konstantin Sergeyevich ended the rehearsal.

"Well, then, *very* good. Do you see how cautiously you must grope for a role? You must spin a fine gossamer cautiously and not produce it all at once. Later you will shape it into a strong rope which will be difficult to break. Continue to work further. Without forcing anything, carefully start from the simplest organic action. For the time being do not think about the character. As a result of your correct actions in the given circumstances, the role, the character will appear. You saw just now, for example, how, cautiously going from one small truth to another, you were able to lay your tracks, to test yourself, to disclose your fantasy and to come to bright, expressive stage action. Work along these lines further. Do you understand what you must do?" he said to the directors. "Come back later and show me again."

It so happened that we didn't have the opportunity to

show this scene to him again. Stanislavski was occupied with other matters. Once he telephone me and asked how Petker's role was developing. Our conversation took about two hours. You could feel his great interest in the role and the new artist. It was very hard for me to answer because my position was a very delicate one. If you told him encouraging things all the time he would stop believing you and, like an investigator, start asking searching questions in order to catch you out; but to talk about mistakes and negative matters—this was to betray one's friend and needlessly trouble Konstantin Sergeyevich.

I dodged as much as possible, but I overdid my answer to his troublesome question about age: "Well, don't worry about that. Petker is doing very well. It is astonishing how he succeeds in showing an old, sick person."

"Hm! . . . Sick? . . . That's terrible, if he is sick. What does it mean 'sick?' Mentally sick? Then it is not interesting. The idea is that Plushkin is possessed by the passion to hoard. Chichikov would be the same at that age. Plushkin has no flexibility in his joints, he can't stand up or sit down quickly, he sees badly, but that's all. For the rest he is perfectly healthy and normal."

"Konstantin Sergeyevich, let us show you our scene once more."

"I will try, but, you see, there is no time. There are other things. I don't know if I can. But please call me and tell me how things are going. You all hide things. Hm . . . Hm. . . . Will you call and really gossip with me sometime? Will you?"

"Of course, Konstantin Sergeyevich."

"Well, then, good-bye."

At Korobochka's

What bliss, when for a few minutes you enter that sphere of your art where it becomes genuine, where you feel true life in the scene! There before you stands your partner, a living person. You see him as someone real; by the expression on his face, by the movement of the pupils of his eyes, you read his thoughts. You, yourself, think completely in character. You allow yourself to take such pauses as are necessary to comprehend this or that situation. Not recognizing any obligation to the audience, you carry on with your partner, or partners, a continuous, delicate and fascinating struggle.

To achieve this is to free the actor from everything which chains him to the level of mediocrity and to bring him to the threshold of the creativity of organic nature—this was the goal toward which all the efforts of Stanislavski were directed.

The part of the landowner Korobochka was given to Stanislavski's wife, Maria Petrovna (Lilina), one of the founders of the Moscow Art Theatre, a wonderful actress who had created a series of sparkling roles. At this time Lilina began to try to play new types and the part of Korobochka was one of the first of these. This was one reason why she had considerable difficulty with the part. An actress with a spontaneous, comic temperament, she played charming women and young girls easily, but she was slightly lost when she tried to portray the old householder. And besides, there was Gogol's style. Her usually unfailing intuition did not help her here. For some reason Maria Petrovna closed all her intuitive approaches to this role, applying what was for her an unusual method of work: a painstaking, corroding analysis with unnecessary reflection and excessive self-control. This killed some of her most valuable qualities: her naïveté and infectious temperament. The words spoken by Stanislavski to one of our other actresses might well have been addressed to Maria Petrovna:

"It is not necessary for you to understand everything in the scene. Meticulousness can be a plague for the actor; he starts to split hairs, to place a mass of unnecessary details between himself and his partner."

Losing her strength and lost in a labyrinth of artificialities and unnecessary complications, poor Maria Petrovna, with each new rehearsal, step by step moved backward from the desired goal. Even Konstantin Sergeyevich with all his genius was not able to save the situation. Maria Petrovna, shocked by her defeat, ceased to understand anything and her work with Konstantin Sergeyevich became almost a reproduction of Gogol's scene between Chichikov and Korobochka.

Stanislavski wittily compared the scene "Chichikov at Korobochka's" to repairing some kind of strange watch mechanism. The watchmaker (Chichikov), knowing his work perfectly, attempts to start the mechanism, but every time it starts, at the last moment, from some unknown cause, the spring noisily unwinds, and everything must be started again. Chichikov, as an experienced craftsman, without losing self-control, patiently begins again to put the mechanism into place, tightens the screws until the crucial moment when a noise is heard and the spring again unwinds completely. Arming himself with patience, Chichikov once again begins his work. This goes on endlessly until, finally out of patience, in an attack of rage he throws the watch on the floor with all his might ... and, unexpectedly, it starts to go. It is as if the mechanism of the watch were in the head of Korobochka. The task of Chichikov consists in penetrating into the interior of this mechanism in order to understand where the fault lies and eliminating the obstacles which are preventing Korobochka from comprehending Chichikov.

Korobochka sincerely wishes to sell her "dead souls"; it would be advantageous to her, but she is afraid of making a bad bargain, thereby losing the opportunity to become rich. She tries to understand not what Chichikov actually says, but what he hides, his "subtext." In the whole scene there is one very simple task for Korobochka—not to be trapped in a bad bargain. To accomplish this it is necessary for Korobochka to "feel out" Chichikov thoroughly, to discover his exact intention. Korobochka, of course, is the foolish blockhead Chichikov called her. However, you cannot act just foolishness. If you act the fruitless activity of Korobochka, her attention to nonexistent difficulties, you will show her foolishness more clearly. Above all it is necessary for the actress to pay genuine attention to the actions of her partner. It seemed that Lilina, even with the help of Stanislavski, could not accomplish this simple thing.

"Isn't it curious," Konstantin Sergeyevich once said, "that a brilliant actress, who is able to play the most delicate nuances, is not able to fulfill this most elementary task?"

Again and again, in all possible ways, he tried to free Lilina from the chains with which she had bound herself by her wrong method of work. But everything was in vain. She was unable to perform even one free, creative action. Everything that she tried to do showed traces of extreme tension. So as not to hold up the performance, Lilina relinquished the part for a time, but continued to work on it without the pressure of an opening. The part was given to Zueva, who played it opening night.

After some time, when the play had been presented many times at the Moscow Art Theatre, Konstantin Sergeyevich invited me to his home for a rehearsal of the scene with Lilina. I went with a light heart; the rehearsal was for Lilina, I was only her partner. My role was established; I had played it many times. To listen to Stanislavski's work on someone else was interesting, instructive and not at all difficult. But it was not to be like that. Konstantin Sergeyevich unexpectedly concentrated all his attention on me. He paid no attention at all to Lilina's first lines, but before I had time to open my mouth, I was stopped by a shout from Stanislavski, which boded no good.

"What *are* you doing?"

"I am shaking the rain off myself."

"In the first place, that's not the way you do it, and furthermore why do you do it in here next to the table? It is not polite in front of one's hostess."

"But he doesn't see the hostess."

"I don't believe it. How can he not see her? It is impossible not to see her."

"At the theatre we have established that mise en scene, but in this room . . ."

"The blocking is not important to me but the logic is! If

today you came in here wet, how would you act under the
given circumstances? . . . Horrible! What are you doing?"

"I . . . want . . ."

"I don't believe anything."

Somehow we got through the beginning of the scene, then
we started the dialogue:

"Some tea, sir?"

"Very well, Mother."

"Terrible! Blah, blah, blah. I don't understand anything."

"Ver—y well, Mo—ther."

"Continue."

"What will you have with your tea, sir? There is fruit
syrup in the bottle."

"That's not bad, Mother, let's drink it with the syrup."

"Ach! Ach! Ach! You have forgotten everything. You say
words but *only words*. How will you behave at the table? She
treats you to tea and a cordial; she is attentive to you, so
respond in the same way. What does it mean to come into a
warm room and be offered tea after being caught in the rain? I
don't see any of that. Well, sir, let's begin."

And the further we went, the more faultfinding Konstantin
Sergeyevich became. He didn't pay any attention at all to
Lilina, who was, it seemed to me, not at her best.

I was in complete despair. I used all my strength in order
to break away from the merciless, hypnotizing gaze of
Stanislavski. I will make one last effort and then I will abandon everything, leave the rehearsal, let come what may. But
suddenly . . . some kind of warm, live intonation came out. I
reached for the decanter, poured out a glass of liqueur,
glanced at Korobochka and saw the clear, attentive eyes of
Lilina. Up to then I had seen her as in a fog, now, suddenly, I
wanted to establish communion with her.

"And what is your name?" I asked. "Excuse me . . . for
making myself so comfortable, but arriving at night . . ."

The apology sounded very sincere. Konstantin Sergeyevich
was silent, and I somehow forgot about him. Only the old lady

sitting opposite interested me. Little by little a pleasant conversation began with her. She told me about her life, complained about her troubles, and somehow everything became interesting. I suddenly got the desire to take advantage of her by buying all her dead souls for fifteen rubles. Since the old lady was evidently not very smart, the matter could be finished off in two minutes.

"Let me have them, Mother."

"What do you mean, let you have them?"

"Simply . . ."

"Yes, but they're dead."

"Who says they are alive? Now you are paying for them, but I will relieve you of the trouble and the payments and, besides, I will give you fifteen rubles. Well then, is that clear?"

"Really, sir, I cannot get it through my head . . ."

I see the eyes of Lilina. They are greedily fixed on me, they glance at the money. I wait for her answer. I do not need words, I see by the pupils of her eyes that doubt is gnawing at her.

"You understand, Mother," I try to explain, "this is money—money doesn't grow on trees. . . . How much did you get for your honey? . . . Well, Mother, you took that sin on your soul!" Lilina is living so truthfully the thoughts of Korobochka, I can read all her intentions without any words from her.

"Well, good, but that was honey. This is just nothing and I will give you not twelve rubles but fifteen just for nothing. And not in silver but in bills."

I see a gleam of understanding in the eyes of Maria Petrovna. Now the matter will work out successfully. But suddenly:

"No, I am still afraid of making a bad bargain."

The spring unwound with a crash. I sat down opposite Maria Petrovna and tried to decide the best way to approach her. I heard an explosion of laughter from those at the rehearsal. Not paying any attention to it, I started again to work on

Korobochka. But the moment I made contact with her through my eyes and was ready to conclude the matter, I almost burst into laughter myself. I suddenly saw Lilina before me embodying Gogol's old woman in an extremely droll way. Her eyes, slightly frightened but full of curiosity, were riveted on me with an expression of impenetrable stupidity. She was so serious in her reactions to me, my actions and thoughts, that I had to make a great effort to control myself and become as serious as she.

The scene proceeded smoothly. We put questions to each other, tried to guess each other's thoughts and intentions, tried to trick each other, to frighten, to convince, to arouse pity; we attacked each other with frenzy, retreated, rested and again entered into the struggle. In all our actions there was logic and expediency as well as a conviction that everything that was taking place was of importance. Our attention was only on our partner; we did not think about the audience. The question of whether we were playing well did not interest us at all. Each of us was occupied with his own business. I had to make the very complicated and incomprehensible mechanism which was located in Korobochka's head work at any cost. I was aiming only for that. We didn't do anything extraordinary; everything was simple, without any comic tricks. Nevertheless, the small audience, with Stanislavski at its head, was literally falling off the chairs with laughter. It seems to me that at that moment we were very close to Gogol. Here was that grotesque to which nobody could object, not even Stanislavski.

"So what happened?" said Konstantin Sergeyevich at the close of the rehearsal. "You were carried away on the wave of intuition and you played the scene excellently. This is most valuable in art; without this there is no art. You will never be able to play this scene that way again. You may play worse, you may play better, but what you just did—that cannot be repeated and is for this reason priceless. Try to repeat what you played and nothing will happen. This cannot be fixed. You can only fix those paths which led you to this result. I tortured you, Vasily Osipovich, so that you would search for the sense of truth in the simplest physical actions. This leads to the awakening of intuition. I pushed you toward the path of the simplest logical sequence of action, toward the path of genuine, organic communion. After you became aware of their logic, you believed in your actions and started to live genuine organic life on the stage. Each actor must discover this way for himself. It is inescapable and indispensable. It is the means to awaken one's intuition. Follow this path, keep it constantly in mind. You need do only this and the result will come of itself."

"And Maria Petrovna?"

"Maria Petrovna simply began to be interested in our work, in the process of 'enlivening' Toporkov. Having become interested, she really gave him her attention. This is true concentration on an object. This freed her from everything which was disturbing her, from all the fetters which bound her, and led her into living communion with a living person. Here one influenced the other ... some kind of explosion occurred and from it came this quality of genuineness."

It now became clear to me why Konstantin Sergeyevich had turned his attention toward me and had completely ignored Maria Petrovna, for whom the rehearsal had been called. This was a special approach to the individuality of the actress.

Much later, at one of the rehearsals of *Tartuffe*, Konstantin Sergeyevich said:

"Many people know the system, but very few are able to apply it. I, Stanislavski, know the system, but I am still not able, or, more accurately, I am only beginning to be able, to apply it. In order to master what has been worked out in our system, I would have to be born a second time and after living sixteen years, begin my acting career all over again."

CHAMBER SCENE

In the play there is a so-called "Chamber Scene" where frightened, depressed functionaries assemble in the house of the Public Prosecutor for a conference called because of the scandalous rumors about Chichikov circulating all over the town which threaten unpleasant consequences. I was not in this scene, if you don't count one line spoken behind a door, so I was able to observe Stanislavski's directing in all its subtlety. This was perhaps the best scene in the play. Here the character of those who had participated in Chichikov's strange, incomprehensible venture was revealed. This is a comparatively short but very bright scene. In it are concentrated Gogol's most vivid ideas and situations. If in the first stages of the work on this play we had tended toward exaggerations of every kind, in this scene the directors Sakhnovsky and Telesheva were even more zealous in their search for striking forms. Their obvious wish was to surpass Gogol himself. But no matter how they struggled, no matter how many solutions they invented, not one of them was successful; they only exhausted the actors. That which in Gogol sounded so convincing, so truthful and so revealing became in performance greatly exaggerated. Externally it had pretensions to brightness and sharpness, but inwardly, in essence, it was cold, empty and unconvincing. The actors didn't believe anything they expressed on the stage.

In starting work on the Chamber Scene, Stanislavski first of all criticized the exaggerated external methods of the actors and pointed out their lack of logic.

"Why do you make such faces when you come into the room?"

"That is from fear . . . we are frightened by the events."

"You cannot play 'fear'. You have to save yourself from a specific danger; that danger is not here in this room, but out there where you came from. In this room there are no strangers, but you continue to be afraid. You show no logic in your actions. Instead of being relieved, you try to *play* fear, and so tastelessly exaggerated. It is possible to discover sharp forms only through the logic and consistency of your behavior. If I do not believe your logic, you won't convince me of anything, even though you walk on your hands or glue on five noses and eight eyebrows. I once saw a splendid vaudeville actor take off his trousers and hit his mother-in-law with them. It was wonderful and did not shock anyone because the actor was able to convince the audience of the logic of his behavior; there was nothing else to do but to act in that way. He prepared us for that, step by step. Do you want to find an effective form? First, find the correct content: genuine human feelings and logical, consistent action; then gradually develop all that to the limit of effectiveness."

In the work on this scene, Konstantin Sergeyevich proceeded in a completely opposite direction from the one in which we had been going. There was no exaggeration, no overacting. Every action that was more than called for was rooted out.

"What are you doing with that handkerchief?"

"I am wiping my forehead."

"What for?"

"He [the character] was so frightened he was perspiring, so . . ."

"Nobody wipes his forehead that way; that's overacting. You are not wiping your forehead, you are *playing* fear again. Try to *really* wipe your forehead."

This part, in which all the participants of the scene were involved, went on for a long time. Finding fault with one thing or another, Stanislavski stopped for a long time on what seemed to us trifles, on simple physical actions, which seemed to have no special meaning until the actors carried out each to its fulfillment. Konstantin Sergeyevich purposely brought to the rehearsal a study of the very simplest elements of the actor's technique. Nowhere else had he been quite so exacting in the application of his method.

The scene finally became bright and spirited, but what

complicated, fine work Konstantin Sergeyevich had put into it! Three clerks enter, one by one. How long Stanislavski worked on each entrance!

"Remember, a threat is hanging over you. You are bound together by a common danger. Look to one another for safety. When you come in, you are among your own people and you can rest easy. Remember this and do not play more than is necessary, do not overact anything. You just come in and see that all here are your friends. Relax your muscles! Try it! . . . No, not that! The entrance of each clerk should be a scene in itself. You make your way under fire the whole distance to the threshold, but as soon as you cross it, you are relatively free from danger. Look for assurance in the eyes of each person present, just as they are looking for it in yours. Do only this and don't add anything. The through-line-of-action of each person is to find a way out of the difficulty. What does this mean? Each as he comes in quickly joins the others and makes an appraisal of the eyes of his companions. Don't take your eyes off one another."

The actors gradually started to "see" and began to genuinely understand the essence of the clerks' commotion. The atmosphere of a conspiracy began to be felt. The players began to believe in themselves, in their actions; truth was created. This was good to see, but still it did not go beyond the limits of an etude. The work proceeded.

The Chief of Police came on the stage. He had been at the inn where Chichikov was staying. Everyone rushed to him.

"Well?"

"He is rinsing his mouth with milk and figs." °

"Horrible!" interrupted the voice of Stanislavski. "You have destroyed everything that has been built up. I didn't understand anything that you said."

"He is rinsing his mouth with milk and figs."

° At the time, considered a beneficial and effective mouth wash and gargle.

"What important news you have brought! 'He is rinsing his mouth with milk and figs.' How do you evaluate this—as a positive or a negative occurrence? You haven't decided yet, but you start to talk. Ah, ah, ah! Well now, where did you come from with this news?"

"From the inn."

"Well, tell us how you entered the inn; how you organized things there. Tell us how you spied on him, and so forth."

"I ... arrived at the inn ... inquired in what room Chichikov was staying ... and then, through the keyhole, I saw Chichikov rinsing his mouth."

"That's all? My God, what poverty of imagination! This is a whole series of events: the Inspector is tracking down a criminal. Imagine! He must work out the whole plan; he must arrange with the innkeeper to get into the inn without anybody seeing him. You can imagine what commotion this would lead to. You might even need a disguise. A lot of little things might happen. Think it over thoroughly. How many different adventures there could be! To get this valuable information about Chichikov's rinsing his mouth with figs cost the Inspector a great deal of effort, talent, inventiveness and cleverness. If you truly visualize all this, then, when you bring the Inspector onstage, you will not mumble, you won't give the news as if it were nothing—as you have just done. You are not bringing the past onto the stage—you don't know what it is—you don't have it. Listen, this is important for everyone: Each one has to know very well not only what is taking place on the stage, but also what has taken place before and what will follow. Naturally, if you do not know this you cannot be convincing in what you are playing. It is all intermingled.

"An unbroken film of images like a motion picture must be created in your mind. If this doesn't exist, you cannot play the fragmented scenes convincingly. Well, now, try to tell me how the Inspector acted at the inn."

Konstantin Sergeyevich subjected each of the players to a thorough treatment, applying whichever of his prescriptions was necessary to achieve an unlimited, organic quality in the player's acting. There was no question of anything grotesque or exaggerated. He wanted only logic and truth in the fulfillment of their actions. Little by little the scene in the Prosecutor's chamber came to life.

The frightened clerks moved around the room as if out of their minds, grasping at one or another suggestion and immediately rejecting it. The slightest noise, the screeching of the parrot frightened them. In such a panic they were ready to believe anything about the mysterious activities of Chichikov; if only they knew the truth, they could shield themselves from disaster.

The earnestness which Stanislavski succeeded in stimulating in the actors was the scene's most valuable quality; this produced its humor. It was for the sake of this that the laborious and painstaking exercises had been undertaken. The results were striking; what a wonderful foundation for the scene that was to follow, where Nozdrov enters the room joyfully, a little bit drunk. Not only does he not meet with the distrust usually accorded him, on the contrary, the clerks unwittingly begin to encourage him in his lies. They watch him eagerly to catch his every word. How could one help exaggerating? What a contrast to the first scene, "An Evening at the Governor's," where everyone was stepping aside, trying as much as possible to avoid any kind of contact with Nozdrov! Now everything was different: Nozdrov talked, they listened. They even prompted him with material for his lies.

"Was he a counterfeiter?"

"He was."

"Wasn't Chichikov a spy?"

"He was."

"It is terrible to think, but wasn't it rumored that Chichikov was Napoleon?"

"Napoleon!"

What freedom for Nozdrov! How he bathed in this atmosphere of unprecedented attention! How easy it was for

Moskvin, responding to this real attention, to fling to the clerks Gogol's marvelous lines! This genuine interplay of the clerks and Nozdrov riveted the audience's attention on what was happening on the stage.

The player of Nozdrov doesn't have to "play" anything, he is being brought out by the others. And it is not necessary that he be very drunk; that would not be so interesting. Nozdrov was in that early state of drunkenness in which God knows what lies are told. It is not surprising that he became expansive and flourished in the unusual atmosphere of confidence and attention that surrounded him.

THE BALL AT THE GOVERNOR'S

Working on the main scene, "The Ball and Supper at the Governor's," Konstantin Sergeyevich attempted to further strengthen the through-line-of-action of the "hero" of the play.

The Ball and Supper at the Governor's is almost a pantomime; the text is really insignificant. There is the possibility here for great directorial development: the creation of sharply outlined genre pictures of a provincial ball of splendor and magnificence. Konstantin Sergeyevich avoided such a solution, making the whole act properly unpretentious in order not to divert the attention of the audience from the hero of the play—Paul Ivanovich Chichikov—who might become lost among the other guests. The ball and supper must be only a background which emphasizes the hero. There, before the eyes of the whole assembly, he will fall from the heights of his glory.

At the opening of the curtain, the audience sees a room in the Governor's house; music is heard. The older guests, men and women, are sitting in armchairs and on divans in the foreground; in the background young people are dancing, but the ball is not yet at its height. Here and there groups of guests begin to come alive. Evidently, some sort of news is being passed around.

Gradually, the gaze of everyone turns to one point, to the entrance of the room where, to everyone's joy, appears Paul Ivanovich in brilliant evening dress and beautiful gloves. He moves from one group to the other, meeting everywhere the most cordial reception. Each movement of Chichikov's is noted. Each of the ladies tries adroitly and without being noticed to pin a cotillion favor on his coat. By the time he, in fascinated conversation with the Governor's daughter, is going in to supper, his coat is covered with glittering trinkets. Even in the large ballroom and in the midst of the gaily dressed crowd of guests at the table, Chichikov does not for one moment escape the attention of the audience, notwithstanding the fact that he, in essence, doesn't do anything; the others "act" upon him. The brilliance of the ball, the abundant supper, the splendid ladies and gentlemen—all that is of secondary importance. In the foreground is always Paul Ivanovich Chichikov, and therefore the ball and the supper continue the development of the intrigue of the play and hold the attention of the audience.

The beginning of our work on this act was somewhat unusual. Stanislavski started by working out the general rhythm of the guests' comportment; like the conductor of an orchestra, he required the actors seated at the table to vary their behavior in accordance with widely differing rhythms. Several rhythmical units were established, beginning at a point where there was no movement, from "silent" position, to the point of maximum activity. About twenty actors are sitting at the table carrying on quiet conversations; their voices are low and velvety. This is rhythm number 1. Rhythm number 2 is almost the same, but the voices sound a little higher in pitch. In rhythm number 3, the voices sound still higher and the tempo is faster; the listeners already are beginning to interrupt those talking. With rhythm number 4, the voices rise still higher and the tempo not only gets faster, but becomes somewhat broken; the listeners no longer pay attention to what is being said but only look for an opportunity to interrupt the speaker. In rhythm number 5, most of the guests are talking at the same time without listening to one another; their voices are high-pitched and the tempo of their speech is jumping and syncopated. Rhythm number 6 has the highest sound level and the maximum syncopation. No one listens to anyone, each seeks only to be heard. In truth, the whole thing was more like an exercise in music than a rehearsal in acting. All of it was remarkable and fascinating. Everyone was involuntarily caught up in the common rhythm; everyone submitted to its fascination and found ways to justify it.

Up to this time I had some understanding of rhythm, but now for the first time I experienced it with clarity and concreteness. It surprised me how what seemed to me mechanical exercises could give rise to such organic, subtle human behavior of such varied colors. But it would be a mistake to think that you can come to such a result easily; to do this, you have to move through the entire range of rhythm. Later I often saw tense moments on the stage achieved by purely outward rhythm, but, if this remained only *external*, it never produced the required effect. The ability to lead the actor to an inner justification of a rhythm is one of a director's most difficult jobs. Failing this, a director is merely imposing conventional solutions.

Working further on the staging of the Governor's ball, Konstantin Sergeyevich gave much time to perfecting the purely *outward* behavior of the participants in the scene: how a servant should bring in and serve food to a guest; how a gentleman should ask a lady to dance, place a chair for her, take her in to supper; how the guests should eat, clink glasses, drink; how they should hold a knife and fork, etc. Sometimes Stanislavski struggled for hours on one of these seeming trifles, trying to get from the actor accuracy, adroitness and expediency in carrying out these simple actions. He wouldn't relax until the manners of the player conformed perfectly to the style of the epoch and the image of the character. Working in this way, Stanislavski finally created that precise system by which his actors were able to create their splendid improvisations, which over the course of many years preserved the brightness and freshness of their performances.

In talking to the players on the opening night of *Dead Souls,* Konstantin Sergeyevich said:

"I will permit the performance to go on, even though it is not yet ready. It is not yet *Dead Souls,* not Gogol, but I see in it living shoots of Gogol's play. Follow the path you are on and you will find Gogol—but that will not be soon."

He said to me:

"You have only just recovered from your 'sickness.' You have learned to walk and act a little. Strengthen your alive but still weak line-of-action. In five or ten years you will be able to play Chichikov, and in twenty, you will be able to understand Gogol."

The critics seriously reproached us for our production. Naturally, we could not give the immortal poem the treatment it deserved, but who could? The aesthetes compared us to one of the theatres dedicated to formalism and maintained that its actors could fulfill this difficult task more brilliantly.

Time showed the error of their judgment. That formalistic theatre went out of existence long ago. The Moscow Art Theatre's production of *Dead Souls,* in which live sprouts of genuine art had been carefully nurtured, continued to grow, as had been predicted by Stanislavski, and remained in the repertory for many years, enjoying uninterrupted success with its audiences.

Understanding the influence of *everything* on the creativity of an actor, Konstantin Sergeyevich vigilantly took note of all that which had a good or bad influence on his actors outside the walls of the theatre. He was always eager to help an actor in a difficult moment and this applied not only to the principal actors, but to the young people in minor roles.

During the time when I was manager of the troupe, I frequently had to talk with Konstantin Sergeyevich about our actors. These conversations often took place on the telephone. Perfectly understanding each actor, he knew in what way and to what degree he was useful to the theatre and in our talks he tried to pass this knowledge on to me.

"In order to create the highest art, colors of the most diverse tints and nuances are needed. Some of them will be used only in rare cases, but it is necessary to keep them at hand. The Moscow Art Theatre must do this too; this troupe is our palette. Each actor has his value as a special, inimitable color. We must treasure him, no matter how humble a place he occupies. It would not be easy for us to find a substitute for him. He has been brought up within the walls of this theatre; he has been infused with its spirit.

"It is your responsibility to be concerned about that most valuable asset of our theatre, that without which the theatre cannot exist—the actor. This concern must be not only for the great important questions, but also for all the trifles which are related to the actor's life. Do you realize what a responsibility lies upon you?"

Dissatisfied with contemporary acting technique, Stanislavski worried about the future of the Moscow Art Theatre and used every meeting with his actors and directors to instill in them his new ideas. Each of his rehearsals invariably turned into an experiment in the nature of the actors' creativity. His strength was more and more directed toward the end that not only should the actors understand and master his method, but that the directors should also understand and apply it. To do this, they must be able to "get into the actor's skin." So the idea of a performance where the roles would be played exclusively by directors was initiated; I saw the first rehearsal.

About ten directors, among them Sakhnovsky, E. S. Telesheva and N. M. Gorchakov, gathered in the rehearsal hall in Leontyev Lane. There were also observers, among whom were

N. V. Yegorov, treasurer of the Theatre, Konstantin Sergeyevich's secretary, R. K. Tamantseva, and several actresses
and actors of the Theatre.

The company took their places around the big table and
waited with excitement for the entrance of Stanislavski. This
was in the spring of 1938, several months before his death. He
did not feel well; his strength was leaving him and he had only
just recovered from grippe. The eyes of everyone were directed toward the door through which Stanislavski would appear. It was quite late in the afternoon; in the twilight a
strange group appeared: at first a nurse in a white uniform,
then the tall, stooped figure of Stanislavski with his snow
white hair. Supported under the arms and moving his legs
with difficulty, Stanislavski went to the table, greeted everyone with a bow and took his place.

"Well now, what do you plan to play?" he asked the
directors after a short conversation on general topics.

"Well, we would like to try Gogol's *Marriage.*"

"*Marriage?* Oh, oh, oh! Why did you choose such a difficult
play? Well . . . it's all the same. Please begin."

I once read an unfinished satirical novel by a talented
Soviet dramatist, now dead. In it the young writer tells about
his struggle with the production of his first play; he implies it
was at the Moscow Art Theatre.

A rehearsal is described in which the main director is
recognizable as Stanislavski. A love scene was being shown,
the acting of which pleased the young author very much. The
dramatist was surprised that this beautiful scene did not satisfy
the director who, seeing it, said something like:

"Horrible! This is a love scene! But you do not love your
lady at all. Do you know what love is? It means everything for
her. Do you understand? 'I sit for her, I walk for her. Whatever I do, I do for her.' Is that clear?"

Then suddenly:

"Prop men!!"

The frightened prop men ran onstage.

"Bring a bicycle."

This unexpected request completely stunned the inexperienced dramatist and the actor/lover. When they brought the bicycle, the director suggested to the actor, who had turned pale, that he ride around his beloved on the bicycle.

"But you must do this for her, do you understand? Only for her."

"But I don't know how to ride a bicycle, I absolutely . . ."

"But for her you *must* know. Now then, please."

The author evidently had thought that in this request he was cleverly and pointedly ridiculing the directing methods of Stanislavski. However, in spite of some exaggerations which gave the incident a ludicrous character, the method of work described by the author was typical of Stanislavski.

Something similar to what was described in the novel took place at the rehearsal with the directors. Stanislavski suggested to those present that they perform a simple exercise:

"Please . . . each one of you write a letter. Do this with imaginary articles, but pay attention to every detail: how you pick up a pen, move the inkwell toward you; how you open the ink bottle, check how much ink is left, how you take paper, etc. The more details, the better. Do not hurry, do the exercise fully; do everything for yourself, not to show."

Konstantin Sergeyevich vigilantly followed the carrying out of the exercise, involving in the work not only the players but *all* who were present. He found fault with many little things, several times demanding that the action be repeated again and again and, for some reason, specified that the exercises be directed chiefly to Yegorov, the treasurer of the Theatre, who was there simply out of curiosity!

Stanislavski's intention was undoubtedly to apply new experimental methods so we could not even guess how the work on *The Marriage* would develop. It had begun with exercises in the simplest physical actions which, seemingly, had no relationship to the subject of the play. This was to be the first and only rehearsal; the condition of his health and other circumstances did not permit Konstantin Sergeyevich to continue.

Tartuffe

Stanislavski's last work, which unfortunately he did not live to complete, was on Molière's *Tartuffe*. In this play he used a small group of actors from the Moscow Art Theatre. His aim was a pedagogical one; therefore, it would be more accurate to call it not work on a play, but work on perfecting the technique of actors engaged in a play.

During the course of his whole life, Stanislavski was concerned with perfecting the way for an actor to work on himself and his role. He considered an advance of even one step in the technical preparation of the actor of great importance toward the fulfillment of his creative tasks.

Daring directorial conceptions which could not be justified by the actors were rejected by him. Better something simpler within the capability of the actor than a fruitless rush to unattainable heights by unjustified means.

A director's plan, which is not fulfilled by the actors, remains a plan, not a performance. We can appreciate the director's imagination, but such a production can never touch the heart of the audience.

Stanislavski tried to embody the stage images of Molière's immortal work with the help of a new, more perfect and convincing actor's technique. He considered it especially urgent for the Soviet theatre to master the classics; the traditional presentations of *Tartuffe* and the mediocre methods of playing it did not satisfy him, by any means.

In order to make possible more productive work and a more successful accomplishment of his intention, Stanislavski asked that the group of actors he had chosen for the work on *Tartuffe* be relieved of all work in the Theatre, with the exception of those with parts in the current repertory.

One of the reasons for the choice of the play was that it had a small cast and the Theatre would not suffer because of their absence. Another reason was that Stanislavski wanted to show that his method was universal, not limited to what is sometimes thought the "typical" Moscow Art Theatre repertory—Chekhov and the like. Moreover, the play pleased Stanislavski very much. As we know, he had once before begun work on a production of *Tartuffe,* but for some reason had not finished it.

In the group which worked on the play were Kedrov in the role of Tartuffe; Knipper-Chekhova and Bogoyavlenskaya who shared the role of Mme. Pernelle; Koreneva as Elmire; Gerot, Cleante; Bendina, Dorine; Bordukov, Damis; Mikheyeva as Mariane and Kislyakov as Valere; I played Orgon.

As it turned out, Knipper-Chekhova, for several reasons, could not take an active part in this work so the role of Mme. Pernelle passed to Bogoyavlenskaya. Later, after *Tartuffe* had been presented many times at the Moscow Art Theatre, Knipper-Chekhova played the part several times.

Bordukov left the group and was replaced by A. M. Komissarov, but this happened much later, after the death of Stanislavski, when the mounting of the production had passed completely into the hands of Kedrov. Bogoyavlenskaya and I, besides playing roles, aided Kedrov in the work of directing. Bogoyavlenskaya worked with the young people, and I directed the scenes in which Kedrov was occupied as an actor.

At the first meeting, Konstantin Sergeyevich talked with each one of us about the character of the work, about our interrelationships, our communion with each other.

"If you are interested only in the chance to play a new part with a slightly renovated technique, I can tell you in advance, you will be disappointed. I absolutely do *not* intend to stage a production; laurels for directing do not interest me at this time. Whether I stage one production more or less does not matter, but it is important that I hand on to you everything which I have stored up throughout my life. I want to teach you how to play not one part, but many. I urge you to consider this seriously. The actor must work on himself, on the perfecting of his skills all the time. He must do this in order to master all roles, not just the one he is studying.

"I beg you to ask yourself: Do I really wish to learn? Please be sincere. There is nothing to be ashamed of; you are mature people, each of you has earned the name of actor; each of you has the right to count himself a master and may expect to spend the rest of his life in this profession. The possibility of playing two or three brilliant roles in the theatre may attract you more than the prospect of long, difficult training with me. I fully understand this. If that is the case, have the courage to acknowledge it; I will have more respect for your honest recognition of this than for any pretended interest in this work. But I must warn you that without such study, you will come to a blind alley.

"The art of the Moscow Art Theatre is such that it demands of its actors constant renewal, constant, persistent work. It is built on the reproduction and transmission of live, organic life; it does not tolerate static forms and traditions however beautiful. It is *alive* and like everything alive must have uninterrupted development and movement. What was good yesterday, will not serve today; today's performance will be different from that of tomorrow's. Such an art demands a special technique—not a technique of fixed methods, but a technique for mastering the laws of the creative nature of man. With the understanding of these laws comes the ability to influence this nature, to control it, to discover at every performance one's own creative possibilities, one's own intuition. This is artistic technique or, as we'll call it, psychotechnique. This technique lies at the foundation of the art of our theatre and sets it apart from other theatres. Our art is beautiful, but, I repeat, it demands constant, persistent work on oneself. Otherwise, more quickly than you think, the technique will degenerate and turn into nothing; our theatre will then descend to a level lower than the common, mediocre theatres. Definitely lower, because in those theatres there is a firm mastery of the clichés of external acting and there are established traditions which have been handed down from generation to generation. These will suffice to support a theatre of a certain quality, but our art is very fragile and if those who create it do not take continual care of it, do not move ahead, do not develop, do not perfect it—it will quickly die.

"The desire to master this technique must inspire everyone in our theatre, actors and directors alike. Our art is a collective one. Individual actors, however brilliant, will not suffice. We must consider a play as a unit, a harmonious combination of all its elements, a complete artistic production.

"Departing this life, I want to leave with you the foundation of this technique. It is not possible to express it in words; it must be assimilated through practical work. If we achieve good results in this work and you grasp this technique, you will be able to propagate it and develop it further.

"I want to give you a clue: The essence of the system consists of these commandments which will give you a correct approach to all roles.

"Remember: Every exacting actor, however great, at certain intervals, say every four or five years, must go back and study anew. It is also necessary for him periodically to place his voice—it changes with time. He must also rid himself of those habits which have adhered to him like dirt, as for example, coquetry, self-admiration, etc. As an artist, it is necessary for him constantly to widen his culture.

"Now, do you understand the task which confronts you? I repeat once more: Do not think of performance—think only of training, training, training. If you agree to study, let's begin; if you don't want to, let's part without hard feelings. You will go to the theatre to continue your work, and I will gather another group and do what I consider my duty to art."

Practical studies began later. In the beginning they were led by Kedrov, under the direct supervision of Stanislavski and bore a special character. But I will come to that later.

It is well known that Stanislavski felt that the future of the Moscow Art Theatre lay in the further development and strengthening of its origins in realism. He felt that realistic art, which truthfully reflects the "life of the human spirit," was capable of affecting an audience, of educating it. In order to manifest his ideas about realism, Stanislavski constantly searched for striking, truly organic embodiment. To accomplish this, he had, above all, to free the actor from those theatrical clichés which hide his living, human spirit from the audience.

"I cannot play any role," said Stanislavski, "until I have freed my creative spirit from the old clichés. In work one must always start from oneself, from one's own natural quality and then continue according to the laws of creativity. One must take into consideration the logic of the role.

"Art begins when there is no role, when there is only the 'I' in the given circumstances of the play. If one 'loses oneself in the role,' one is looking at the role from the outside, one is copying it. Working according to our system one may act correctly and well or correctly and badly, but one will not act correctly externally as, for instance, Coquelin did.

"To play correctly externally is very difficult. Perhaps it is good; but the art of Coquelin impresses you only at the time you are watching him, the art of Yermolava enters into your heart, into your life. The actor really acts and lives his own feelings: he touches, smells, listens, sees with all the finesse of his organism, his nerves; he truly acts with them."

Stanislavski gave his actors the ability to experience stage events spontaneously.

"My method helps the actor to become fascinated with the sensations of the moment. You were praised for a certain piece of your acting, for a gesture, for an intonation. Do not make too much of them, do not cherish them; change them for more interesting ones and avoid clichés. Take a sponge and erase them."

One cannot say that Stanislavski brought something completely new to his last work, something contrary to his pervious concepts; this will be evident from the description of the *Tartuffe* rehearsals. But in his work on the method of physical actions, Stanislavski gave his system greater concreteness.

At that time he considered the foundation of his system to be the work on physical actions, and he brushed away all that might distract the actors from its significance. When we reminded him of his much earlier methods, he naïvely pretended that he didn't understand what we were talking about. Once someone asked:

"What is the nature of the 'emotional states' of the actors in this scene?"

Konstantin Sergeyevich looked surprised and said:

" 'Emotional states' What is that? I never heard of it."

That was not true. At one time this expression had been used by Stanislavski himself. Nevertheless, in this case, he kept us from fixing our attention on it and directed us to the desired channel. He was afraid of all backward glances which could interfere with reaching his goal.

When one of the actresses told him that she had kept detailed notes of all the rehearsals in which she had taken part under his direction and now didn't know how to use this treasure, Stanislavski answered: "Burn them all."

The most convincing quality of our art is its sincerity. Anything sincerely said or done never arouses doubt. Sincere laughter is always contagious; false, artificial laughter is repulsive. Sincere tears always touch you, but you will never believe the grief feigned by false tears. Sincerity—this is the charm of a person. The actor who has sincerity on the stage cannot help being charming; it is impossible to separate this quality from his creativity. We know many actors who are charming in life, who possess beautiful external qualities and have lovely voices, but whose charm disappears as soon as they appear on the stage.

The ability to be sincere onstage—that is talent.

What quality unites all our great actors? The sincerity of their stage behavior. In what was the greatness of Varlamov? What did his inimitable humor consist of? His stomach, his fat legs, his grotesque figure, his voice? Definitely not. There were other actors who were not inferior to him in their outward qualities. However, in the whole history of the theatre, Varlamov was unique, his talent was unsurpassed. This talent enabled him to manifest completely his dramatic imagination. Strelskaya also possessed such a quality. When these two great actors met on the stage they created a miracle. They erased the boundary between the stage and life. Performing often in shallow, foolish comedies and vaudeville scenes, they won their audiences with the sincerity and truthfulness of their performance. This quality, this talent, was given to those actors with such lavishness that it allowed Varlamov, although he never worked on himself during his whole life, to have, nevertheless, a brilliant career. Had he mastered the other techniques which are necessary to an artist, he could have been, undoubtedly, even greater. Davydov once said: "Give me the talent of Varlamov and I will conquer the whole world." What Varlamov possessed was indeed valuable if that alone could bring him such praise.

Stanislavski demanded of his actors a sense of truth, the ability to give themselves to the events of the play easily and with complete sincerity, to follow the logical line of their actions continuously, to believe the other actors' logic as well as their own. These qualities, which Varlamov possessed by intuition, may be acquired by other actors only by persistent work.

Stanislavski warned us many times against a cold, intellectual approach to creativity. He demanded action from us, not discussion.

"When the actor is reluctant to show his will, when instead he hesitates to create and begins to reason too much, he is like a horse stamping in place because he lacks the strength to move his load. In order to act without inhibition the actor should not mark time; rather, he should become fascinated with the action. If I want to act, I act boldly. Action comes from the will, from the intuition; discussion comes from the mind, from the head. The purpose of my system is to open the way to the creativity of the organic nature of the actor, especially at those times when nothing turns out well."

As far back as our work on *The Embezzlers,* he had directed our attention to the importance of control, clarity and completeness in even the most insignificant physical actions. This was done to an even greater degree in the work on *Dead Souls.* In the last period of his activity, that is to say in the work on *Tartuffe,* Stanislavski considered this element, physical actions, of paramount importance.

One must not think, however, that the work on physical actions and the other technical methods of Stanislavski were ends in themselves, as they often became for some ungifted followers of his system. Every technical device of Stanislavski's served only as an auxiliary to the achievement of the main objective—*the fullest embodiment of the stage character.* The choice of the physical actions is always dictated by the given circumstances and the final intention.

It would be a mistake as well to regard physical action as only bodily movement. Real, expedient action, which is directed to the achievement of some objective, in the moment of fulfillment will without fail turn into psychophysical action.

When working with us on *Tartuffe,* Konstantin Sergeyevich invariably began with the words:

"Well, now, what is the physical line here?"

It was necessary for us to translate the scene into the language of physical actions, and the more simple the action, the better. For example, the crucial scene between Tartuffe and Elmire, with its long monologues, was reduced to very simple physical action: by subtle encouragement, Elmire succeeds in making Tartuffe fall into a trap.

"How will you do this, Elmire? We don't need the text now. Create the scheme of your actions: how you will lure Tartuffe into your net, how you will deal with his advances. In your turn," he said to Kedrov, who played Tartuffe, "regulate your behavior toward Elmire in accordance with that which would be permitted to a respectable woman, the mistress of a house.

"Or let us take another scene, the one in which Orgon is looking for Mariane in order to force her to sign a marriage contract which Elmire, Cleante and Dorine oppose. What is the physical action in this scene?

"Do not speak to me about feeling. We cannot set feeling; we can only set physical action. In this case the action may be defined by the verb 'to hide.' You must hide Mariane from her cruel father. How will you do this? If you do it in a hackneyed way, 'like actors,' you will hide her behind you and look alarmed, but I don't think that would turn out very well. It is most important to *really* hide her."

Stanislavski forbade us to memorize the text; if someone in rehearsal suddenly began to speak Molière's lines, he quickly stopped the rehearsal. To cling to the text, to the exact words of the author, was considered a sign of helplessness in the actor. It was considered the highest achievement if an actor could reveal the scheme of a scene by means of purely physical actions or with a minimum number of words. The words were to play only an auxiliary role.

He forbade us to follow the method of work used in other theatres. At the beginning of our rehearsals, neither learning the text of a role by heart nor the establishment of a mise en scène was permitted. The text was used exclusively to indicate the line of physical actions.

Konstantin Sergeyevich told us repeatedly:

"Without using the text, without a mise en scène, knowing only the content of each scene, if you play everything according to the line of physical action, your part will be at least thirty-five percent ready. First of all, you must establish the logical sequence of your physical actions."

"No matter what kind of delicacy an artist brings to a painting, if the pose of the model breaks physical laws, if truth is not in the pose, if its representation of a sitting figure, say, is not really sitting, nothing will make it believable. Therefore, the painter, before he can think of embodiying the most delicate and complicated psychological states in his painting, must make his model stand or lie down or sit in a way that makes us believe that the model really sits, stands or lies.

"The line of physical actions of a role has precisely the same significance in the art of the actor. The actor, like the painter, must make the character sit, stand or lie down. But this is more complicated for us in that we present ourselves as both the artist *and* the model. We must find, not a static pose, but the organic actions of a person in very diverse situations. Until these are found, until the actor justifies the truth by the correctness of his physical behavior, he cannot think of anything else.

"We must strengthen the line of physical actions," Stanislavski reminded us. "It is sometimes even useful to write them down. Start bravely, not to reason, but to act. As soon as you begin to act you will immediately become aware of the necessity of justifying your actions."

This is the way an actor must approach what Stanislavski called "the art of emotional experience" as distinguished from mere representation. Authentic organic behavior, the sincerity of one's emotional experience, the belief in one's artistic invention—these are the qualities which are truly convincing in the theatre and which win an audience, which influence its heart. These are the qualities which are peculiar to the great masters of the theatre who serve as examples for us.

"It is impossible to possess the role all at once," Konstantin Sergeyevich taught. "There is always much that is vague, not easily understood, difficult to overcome. Therefore, begin with what is clearer, more accessible, with what can be easily established; that is, search for the truth of the simplest physical actions. They will lead you to belief in the "I am", and this will lead you into action, into creativity.

"If the line of physical actions in a role is quite similar to your own given circumstances in life," continued Stanislavski, "if your feelings dry up, there is no cause for alarm; simply return to physical actions and these will restore your lost feelings."

Stanislavski defined the actor as a "master of physical actions." Nothing so clearly, so convincingly transmits the spiritual condition of a person as his physical behavior; that is, as his sequence of physical actions. Not without reason do the most prominent masters of the stage make use of this knowledge. When we recall the successes of Yermolova, Savina, Davydov and Dalmatov, we say in the majority of cases:

"Remember when they said this or that to her, how she nervously took off her gloves, threw them onto the sofa and crossed over to the table?"

Or:

"Remember when her husband wanted to put his cigar butt in the ashtray where she had laid the cigar of her lover, how she quickly substituted another ashtray?

"Remember Duse's playing with the mirror in the last act of *Lady of the Camellias?* "

Countless examples could be brought to mind. Davydov, a master of the art of dialogue and monologue, a genuine virtuoso, invariably at the peak of each of his roles used the "pause for effect." After this, with a few words or even without a single word, merely through a series of subtle physical actions, he revealed to the audience the most secret feelings of the character, his whole essence.

"All our five senses can suggest the most delicate physical actions; you should take note of them and use them when needed," said Stanislavski at one of the rehearsals.

Because he considered physical actions the chief element of stage expressiveness, Stanislavski always demanded clearness and dexterity in their use by his players. He tried to get "good diction" in their physical actions, if it could be so expressed. To achieve this he recommended a daily "toilette" for an actor: exercises with imaginary objects to develop concentration in the actor—a quality so necessary in our art. Each time he repeats these exercises, the actor makes them more complicated; he divides them into small, separate sections and thus develops his "diction" in physical actions.

Signing one's name may seem to be one action, but for the actor-artist even this may involve a hundred and one actions, depending upon differing circumstances. The signing of a paper in itself may have no meaning, and unnecessary details in this simple action can arouse vexation. At another time, this may be for the actor the most interesting moment of his role; then he will need a hundred and one colors for carrying out this apparently simple action.

"Nobody has mastered this technique of physical actions completely, but it is necessary, nonetheless, to continue to strive for it," he said.

In the work on *Tartuffe* no compromises with the rehearsal traditions of the time were permitted. The first step of our rehearsal work might be called "reconnaissance"; it consisted of analyzing the separate scenes as well as the whole play. Kedrov, who led the rehearsals, tried to get a clear and accurate account of the subject of the play from each of the players. The account had to convey just the story line without any unnecessary elaboration. We had only to answer the question: What happened, what took place?

Our account of the story had to be told with the simplicity and lack of affectation of a ten-year-old child.

"A notorious swindler, disguised as a pious man, enters the house of the prosperous bourgeois Orgon, etc."

These statements, varied according to the individuality of the narrator, might be modified in response to questions asked by the director. This work was directed toward determining the required physical actions, the tasks, and the seed of the play. The success of the narrator depended upon his use of a clear, accurate verb to indicate the development of the struggle taking place in the home of Orgon. By this means, the through-line-of-action and counteraction of the play were established. After this was done, it was possible to recognize the factions which were fighting and ask each actor: "Where do you stand in this struggle? What is your position, your strategy, the logic of your behavior?"

This was the first attempt to mark the contours of the future design of the play, the logic of the characters' behavior, the logic of their struggle. The more complicated, the more demanding the rehearsal became, the more it required the actor to examine the material of the role analytically and to deepen his powers of communication and imagination. His account of the play's events must not seem that of an observer, but of a person closely involved in what is taking place. In other words, it should be a "living through" of those events; there should be the desire to interest the listener in their development. In addition to the oral account, we were asked to prepare a written one. In these written accounts the more exact literary form forced us to a deeper penetration and analysis of the actions. In this one's attempts are more important than the results. Even "unsuccessful" attempts in our work are not in vain; their results can appear later, when the actor least expects them.

It is not possible sitting around a table to achieve full understanding of the future design of the part. This is only the first exploration; the process of embodiment is subject to all kinds of changes. This is still the work of the mind, but I fully appreciated its tremendous importance only at the end of the work on *Tartuffe*. For many this may seem naïve, but what about it? Of course the actor must first know the subject of the play, he must define the course of his part. Only then can he rehearse. What is new about that?

The "new" lies in the quality of the work, its thoroughness. To this exploratory period we gave much more time than usual. And it was not spent in vain. Each meeting produced new results. We had never before seen such preparation by the actor for the further steps of the work. The whole story of Orgon's family became clear to each of us in every detail. We began to believe in it as a genuine event; our desire to actualize it on the stage grew stronger.

This unusual method requires of the director vigilance, persistence, the ability to interest the actors and to awaken their imagination. It puts into the hands of the actor material for the most complete development of all the features of the character and permits a more profound expression of the author's idea.

Our later work was characterized by restraint—restraint of our emotions, of our temperament, of our striving for quick results.

"Let's rehearse at once, even if just a little scene."

It seemed to us that we were ready for that; but, no, we were stopped. By this time we were no longer at the table, but, as before, what we did had an unusual character. We had no formal rehearsal space; two floors of the actors' dressing rooms backstage were used. This area had to represent Orgon's home, which had a great many rooms. We were told to establish the location of the principal rooms of the house and distribute the others among the members of the family; this was to be done with all seriousness and efficiency. We were obliged to take into consideration the requirments of a household of ten people of different age, position and character. Where should the dining room, bedrooms, servants' quarters, etc. be placed? The rooms must be comfortable and expediently distributed. Each of us could defend his character's best interests with spirit, but all arguments had to take place in character, as arguments between members of a family. This proved interesting. For a long time we walked with the whole family in the corridors, measured the size of the rooms, drew plans, argued and offered all sorts of possible solutions.

"If the mistress of the house is sick would she be comfortable in the room you have chosen for her? It might be very noisy because of this or that, etc." The bedroom was moved to another place, and as a result other rooms had to be changed. By the end of several rehearsals, we had settled on the disposition of the rooms and had begun to feel at home in them. At the sound of a gong everyone came together in the dining room. Dorine served the dinner, running up and down the stairs. Life went on quietly, peacefully. That is, until the intrusion of Tartuffe.

We acted out such events, for example, as the illness of the mistress of the house and how it affected the behavior of all the inhabitants. Bearing this in mind, the family gathered for dinner and, after dinner, went to their own rooms or out for a walk. Everything was done with concern for that seriously ill person.

We developed other circumstances around events in the play, such as "The Arrival of Tartuffe." Nobody knew yet what kind of person he was, and therefore they accepted him as a man of God. The behavior of Tartuffe, in the beginning, did not call forth suspicion from anyone; he was a model of meekness and humility. Therefore, everyone was well-disposed toward him. Against this background we performed a series of interesting etudes, as for example, "Tartuffe Loses His Self-control" and "The Master of the House Has Gone Mad."

We carried out these episodes with the truth and sincerity of children at play. We enjoyed it. We went to rehearsals gladly and played our games. Sometimes they turned out well and it was satisfying; sometimes nothing worked out and it was vexing and disappointing.

In the world of the theatre other actors and directors gossiped about our work, spread cock-and-bull stories and laughed a great deal. "They are grown-up people, but the devil only knows what trifles they concern themselves with."

And although we continued this work, often with great enthusiasm, all the same, we were not completely confident of its value. Only much later did we understand that this way would lead us to our goal.

Konstantin Sergeyevich said one day:

"A large group of friends is going somewhere on a ship. They are sitting on the deck and eating: they eat, drink, talk, flirt with the ladies. They do all this very well. But is that art? No. It is life. Now take another case: we go to the theatre to a rehearsal. On the stage a deck is built, a table is set, we come onstage and say to ourselves: 'If we came on board ship with a joyous company and had dinner, what would we do?' With this moment our creativeness begins."

Later on, our games in the "home" of Orgon began to build on themes closer and closer to events in Molière's play: "Mme. Pernelle Leaves the House Enraged," or "Orgon and the Marriage Contract."

"Only, for goodness' sake," Stanislavski admonished us, "not a single line of Molière's text, nor any mise en scène."

Having worked on the scene in this manner for some time, we decided to show Stanislavski the results of our efforts. We began with Mme. Pernelle's departure, which is the beginning of the play. The actors, following the general idea of the scene, spoke in their own words. We did not succeed in playing the scene for long; in a very short time, Stanislavski interrupted the rehearsal.

"You are not acting, you are saying words; it is true, they are not the author's words, but you are used to them and they are like a text for you. They sound like a memorized script— only one less perfect than Molière's. For me, what is important here is not your words but your physical behavior. Sit down, please, everyone, and listen attentively. What takes place here according to the physical line? The situation in Orgon's family is extremely tense. The master of the house has gone away, leaving his mother, Mme. Pernelle, to protect Tartuffe. She too worships this 'saintly' person, and if she decides to go away, leaving no one to take Tartuffe's part, what will her son think when he returns? Show how the discord bursts out, how Tartuffe turns it to his advantage and how further struggle with him becomes much more complicated. You must do everything possible in order to hold back, to propitiate this enraged old woman. Mme. Pernelle's stage task is not only *not* to yield to reasoning, but not to allow anyone even to open his mouth. If anyone attempts to argue with her, she must quickly demolish her opponent, insult him and stifle any attempt to continue the struggle. This is Molière, not Chekhov. Here, if there is a scandal, there is a scandal; if there is a fight, there is a fight. They are not playing chess, they're boxing. Well, now, what is the physical line? Determine your behavior. What fascinates you?

"Imagine that there are raging tigers in a cage with the tamer, whom they are ready to tear to pieces at any minute; he holds them back by not taking his eyes off them for even a moment. In their eyes he reads their intention, but he nips it in the bud, not giving them a chance to go into action. If one of the tigers attempts to attack him, he gives him such a lashing that he runs to save himself, with his tail between his legs. Take into account that the tiger is not alone, that there are five or six of them, and each would hurl himself at the tamer if he were to take his eyes off them for a moment. Now then, how would you act? Try it, try it. . . . No . . . none of you is sitting in the correct rhythm! Look for the true rhythm. You, my dear fellow, you are preparing not for a fight, but to rest, to read the paper. [The actor gets up] But no, you need not get up; it is possible to prepare for a jump while sitting. Now, sir, *act*. . . . No, that is not it. I beg each of you, while sitting in your place, to find the true inner rhythm, an agitated rhythm, that expresses itself in small actions. No . . . no, that is all wrong. Really, can't you do such a simple thing? Where is your technique? As soon as your text is taken from you, you lose everything. I want you, above all, to learn to act, to act *physically*. In the future you will need words and ideas to strengthen and develop these actions, but now I urge you simply to prepare yourselves for a fight. Really, is this so difficult?"

For us it was definitely difficult. We could not find what was demanded of us in any way. No matter how much Stanislavski struggled with us, it was without result.

"Ah, ah, ah! The will is missing. This is frightful! You cannot work like this." We tried to assure him that we had the will, that we wanted to resolve the problem, but nothing succeeded. We could not act by sitting in one place. As for "sitting in an agitated rhythm"—somehow it all came out false; we were not true to ourselves, we were confused. We began to think that to do this was altogether impossible.

"Complete nonsense! Rhythm makes itself felt in the eyes, in small movements. These are elementary things. Please, try to sit in a definite rhythm ... change the rhythm of your behavior. A student in his third year should be able to do this."

One of the players, apparently cut to the quick, asked:

"And you, yourself, Konstantin Sergeyevich, are you able to do this?"

We all stood stock still. We waited for the storm, but Stanislavski at once, almost without a pause, quietly answered:

"Of course. You want an agitated rhythm—very well."

And there, seated on the sofa, he was transformed instantly. Before us an extremely perturbed person was sitting as if on hot coals. He took out his watch and, hardly glancing at it, thrust it back again; then he prepared to jump up, but sank down again; he then became completely still, at any moment ready to spring. Without stopping, he made use of a series of very quick movements. Each of these movements was inwardly justified, completely convincing. The spectacle was delightful; we were all spellbound, but he, as if nothing had happened, continued his exercise until, after some time, he calmly asked:

"Do you wish me to continue in another rhythm?"

And he began again. This time he was a completely quiet,

controlled person who apparently intended to lie down to sleep, but had been delayed. It was very convincing.

"But how can *we* do this?"

"Only through daily exercises. Everything that you are doing now is very good, but add to it exercises on rhythm. You cannot master the method of physical actions if you do not master rhythm. Each physical action is inseparably linked with the rhythm which characterizes it. If you always act in one and the same rhythm, then how will you be able to embody a variety of characters convincingly?"

"But, if, as you say, a listless rhythm is peculiar to me," protested the same bold actor, "and we must start with ourselves, with our own qualities, how can I arrive at an agitated rhythm which is completely foreign to me?"

"It all depends . . . if someone steps on your sore corn with his heel, would you remain in your usual languid rhythm?"

"Well, no . . . but here. . . ."

"Your listless rhythm would continue until you were stepped on. In the play there are different circumstances, but the events will affect you just as strongly. Act exactly as you yourself would until you are hurt.

"First, encourage any inclinations to new actions based on your knowledge of physical actions already established. But do not 'perform' them, just find out what they are—'this I may do now, but that, not yet.' Observing the logic, the sequence of the line of physical actions, go over your role using your own words, not the words of the author. Even while studying the text of the play, do not say the words aloud. Work quietly, boldly. Do not stop to criticise yourself: 'Oh, the devil, that's wrong! '

"What does 'actor's faith' mean? An actor must start to act boldly, brightly and logically. The audience will then follow his actions. As he proceeds, he will become fascinated with his work; he has then achieved half the faith. But in order to capture the audience, he must bring this half-faith to full faith."

With this, the rehearsal ended. Stanislavski let us go, not really satisfied with the results of our work. Talking with Kedrov, he complained about our lack of will and even expressed the suspicion that some of us were not at all eager to continue our studies. He felt it necessary to question all of us once more.

To prepare for the next showing, we reviewed all our previous work. We did daily rhythm exercises until it seemed as if we had achieved something. We purposely took another scene, "Orgon and the Marriage Contract." The scene starts with her excited relatives comforting the unhappy Mariane; they discuss how to thwart Orgon's attempt to marry her to Tartuffe. During this stormy discussion, Orgon bursts into the room with the contract in his hand.

Our key words were *"excited* relatives," *"stormy* discussion" and *"bursts."* They indicated the rhythm in which we were to act.

Before beginning the scene, we explained to Stanislavski in detail what we wanted to accomplish, how we had discussed the stressed words, how the relatives planned to give a rebuff to Orgon, etc.

Konstantin Sergeyevich interrupted our discussion.

"When actors start to reason 'we will repulse him, we will do this and that and so forth,' the will is weakened. Don't discuss, just do it. Well, then, how will you act?"

We began to play the scene; not badly we thought.

"What in the world are you doing? A crazy man is running around the house with a knife, searching for his daughter, and you are just deliberating? You must save her! That is true theatrical action. What is the line of physical action here? Decide this first of all. Where can that crazed man burst in from? All your attention must be on the door; not on the door itself, but on its brass doorknob. At the same time try to decide where to hide Mariane. Argue, curse one another, but do not for one second forget the chief object of your attention—the crazy man who is running around the house with a knife. Once he opens the door, it will be too late. The least movement of the doorknob ... and Mariane must be hidden in a moment. Orgon must not suspect that she is here. Now, how would you act?"

Everything, as with all Stanislavski's directions, seemed simple, demanding no further clarification. But once we began to act, we felt how far we were from perfection. Even in our best work we were not doing a hundredth part of what was demanded of us, and even this came through the repetition of more or less clever, but still "theatrical" methods.

"Well, now, forget the play; there is no Orgon, Mariane, or any of the other characters. There is only you, yourselves. Let's play a game. The game consists of the following: Toporkov comes into the corridor and stops some distance from the door. You in this room try to determine exactly where Toporkov is. No one in the room may move from his place until the doorknob moves; as soon as it moves, hide the girl wherever you like, but you must do this before the door is opened and Toporkov bursts into the room. You must not let Toporkov see where you have hidden Mikheyeva. You, Toporkov, coming in, must tell them at once where she is hidden. If you can't, you lose; if you can, then the others lose. Now then, please begin the game, and in the meantime I will talk with the directors."

Konstantin Sergeyevich took off his pince-nez as if to show us that he wasn't watching us, looked at some notes he had made and began to talk with the directors.

We started the game. At first, nothing happened. To hide the girl in such a short space of time seemed impossible. I, Toporkov, burst into the room before they hardly had time to grab her; even if they had hidden her, I would have been able to see where. But gradually, one by one, the players began to get excited. They began to blame each other's clumsiness, they started to scold; they really wanted to win. But I also took measures to win. When one of them said that besides watching for the doorknob to move, they must listen more attentively for the sound of my approaching footsteps, I took off my shoes and played in my socks. We had become so involved in our game that we forgot about Stanislavski and the directors, who had broken off their conversation long ago and were following our excited playing as they might a soccer game. Her family didn't succeed in hiding Mariane; it was too difficult. At the height of the game, Stanislavski interrupted us:

"Well, at last. This is not *theatre;* this is genuine, live action with honest attention and real interest. This is what I need from you in this scene. You still haven't played it adequately, but after today you should be able to understand the fundamental element which lies in the physical behavior of these people. Each one of you must continue to believe in what you are doing, just as you did in this game. In each succeeding rehearsal, search for that same attention, that rhythm, that truth which arose as a result of your genuine fascination with the episode. Don't let the audience distract you; it doesn't exist for you. The more completely you do this, the greater attention they will give to your acting, just as we did now. This is a law of the stage."

Addressing the directors, Konstantin Sergeyevich said:

"Did you notice how spendid, how varied, how unexpected the mise en scène was during the course of these games? You simply cannot invent it in advance. It would be good if you could vary it each time. I dream of a performance where the actors won't know which will be the fourth wall."

Dismissing us, Stanislavski urged each of us to keep in mind everything that had taken place in the rehearsal and to try to perfect what had been done.

"We cannot remember feelings and fix them," he said. "We can just remember the line of physical actions and strengthen it so that it becomes easy and habitual. While rehearsing a scene, begin with the simplest physical actions and make them completely truthful. Search for truth in every trifle. In this way you will arrive at belief in yourself, in your actions. Take into consideration everything that relates to your actions, especially rhythm, which, like everything else, arises as a result of the given circumstances. We know how to perform simple physical actions; depending on the given circumstances these physical actions become psychophysical actions."

The rehearsals of *Tartuffe,* although they had begun with seemingly abstract exercises in separate elements of acting technique, imperceptibly drew nearer to the Molière play. We continued daily scenes and exercises such as the "actor's toilette."

Once the question arose: What are the special methods Tartuffe uses so subtly with Orgon? How does he subdue him, stun him or, as Stanislavski said, "dumbfound" him? Certainly it would be necessary to do something very special to be able to deceive a person like Orgon. If we consider Orgon a simpleton, who could be made a fool of by very simple methods, then the play is not worth doing. No, here we need delicate art. Tartuffe is a dangerous swindler. He is dangerous in that he can outwit far from stupid people; he has an arsenal of varied and subtle means of deluding people which he employs, depending on the victim of the moment.

The first meeting of Orgon with Tartuffe took place in a church, where Orgon was struck with the zeal with which Tartuffe was praying.

"He was praying—now with tender emotion,
Now full of holy fire:
He sighed, groaned, raised his eyes
To heaven reverently, etc."

The hypocrite did it in this way to draw attention to himself.

Take another sharp moment: when Tartuffe, caught in his attempt to seduce Elmire and seemingly without any possibility of justifying himself, comes off unscathed. How does he do it? He has a long monologue in which he throws dust in the eyes of Orgon; it is very difficult to find the truth in such profuse talk, although the evidence is clearly seen. At the height of his fury Orgon asks, "Yes or no?" and Tartuffe boldly answers, "Yes." But all the same Tartuffe comes off unscathed.

How does he do it? One might say that Orgon believes in Tartuffe so much that for him this event is no more than another of his family's intrigues. He would be delighted to believe that Tartuffe seduced Elmire with the loftiest aims. But, naturally, we rejected this. No, Orgon is not such a stupid person. He loves his wife; the evidence against Tartuffe could not be disproved. Orgon believed it and flew into a rage. This complicated Tartuffe's task. He could not get out of this situation by reasoning, naturally; there was no time to talk—that would come later. Here a series of blinding, shocking actions was necessary, but what? We talked a lot with Kedrov about this; we called to mind all the sanctimonious people we had known and discussed the secret of their power over others. We touched upon this in one of the rehearsals with Stanislavski.

"That's exactly right. Try to shock Toporkov so that he will really be shocked."

"How? We know each other too well ... that would be very difficult."

"Why? There's nothing difficult about it. You only have to have courage. Do something outrageous in our presence which you ordinarily would not do before us. Come now, don't think about it. Well, who can?"

But nobody ventured.

"It seems none of you can be impertinent. An actor must have this quality I call impudence."

Half jokingly, half seriously, somewhat confused, we immediately began exercises in impertinence with Kedrov, trying to outdo one another in our boldness. Konstantin Sergeyevich did not stop us, and the exercises continued for quite a long time. The further we went, the bolder we became, the more audacious. Finally we stopped.

"Now then ... very good. There could be limitless variations." After telling us several interesting stories from life

about impudence, he said: "How would you stop an infuriated
man who attacks you determined to kill you on the spot? Very
bold means are necessary, so don't be afraid to resort to them.
Only, please, don't think about the means; just think about
your attacker and decide now how you will stop him. Tomorrow your means may be altogether different. Surprise Toporkov, stun him. Each time shock him in a different way.
Otherwise, he will beat you with his cane."

As a result of these exercises, Kedrov, who was playing
Tartuffe, made a great "find" in his scene with Orgon in the
third act of the play. Caught and exposed, Tartuffe stands near
the sofa in the middle of the room with a Bible in his hand
and, like a wild animal brought to bay, desperately looks
around for a way out of the situation. With a slow, stealthy
walk, like an enraged panther, Orgon approaches him with his
cane raised to strike and says sarcastically:

"What do I hear, 'my son,'
Are their accusations just?"

After a tense, terrible pause, Tartuffe answers:

"Yes! "

Suddenly, with a shriek, Tartuffe, by a quick push of his
leg, overturns the sofa with a crash. Orgon stands there in
astonished surprise, his cane hanging in midair. The next moment he drops the cane and looks around, not understanding
what has happened. Has the wrath of Heaven punished him
for blasphemy? He looks questioningly at Tartuffe, who is not
paying any attention to him, but is sitting on the floor kissing
Orgon's cane. He seems to be speaking intimately with God,
somewhere above, discussing with Him what to do with
Orgon—to forgive him or to punish him? This strange pose of
Tartuffe's and his incomprehensible conversation with "Someone" could not help making an impression on Orgon, who
becomes more and more confused. Tartuffe, quite aware of all
this, begins to weave the thread of Orgon's thoughts.

"Oh yes, I am very guilty . . ."

Orgon begins to listen to him. He detects in the voice of

this "saint" not only repentance, but outraged innocence. Orgon begins to persuade himself that Tartuffe's "sin" was no more than a response to the provocation of "the enemy," etc.

After warding off the first blow, it was easy for Tartuffe to handle Orgon and to redirect his anger.

At times Konstantin Sergeyevich was saddened by the meager results we showed him after a prolonged period of work. It was not our lack of mastery of a scene that depressed him, but our lack of mastery of the method. Once, after we had played the famous third act scene between Orgon, Dorine and Mariane not, we thought, too badly, Konstantin Sergeyevich didn't even smile and finally said sadly:

"Well, the scene is ready; you can play it at the Moscow Art Theatre. But you could play it this way without having worked with me. I did not bring you together for this. You are just repeating what you have known for a long time; you must move ahead. In order to help you do this, I offer you this method. I thought it would make your task easier, but you refuse it and return to your old ways. Well then, go to the Moscow Art Theatre, they will put on the play for you."

However, one way or another, the time finally came when we could move on to the next step of rehearsal work, a step where the text became necessary. Our improvisations had reached the point where they demanded greater expressiveness through the author's words. This happened by itself, gradually, as a result of an inner need.

Although we rarely went back to the first stages of our work, we continued to carry out the "actor's toilette" before each rehearsal. There were different tasks required now in working on the text. It was still necessary to express the action by an active verb in order to encourage the urge to perform it. We had to join the characters in the play in an active verbal clash. The ground for this had been prepared by our previous work, but the demands of Konstantin Sergeyevich were so great that we suffered not a little embarrassment. He would not permit a single empty sentence; in fact, there could not be a single word unjustified by an inner image.

"You mustn't listen to yourself, but you should see clearly and in minute detail what you are talking about. Then the scene will become clear and the audience will see it plainly."

This concerned the "inside" of the part; as for the outside:

"The characters in a Molière play are Frenchmen, their feelings are very strong. Their thoughts are clear, like the stroke of a pen. They flow quickly and lightly without a pause for explanation. The thought is carried by the whole sentence and it is complicated by the poetic form of the play."

None of us had really mastered the art of reading verse; we did not understand the rhythm of metrical verse. Stanislavski made great demands here:

"The rhythm of the verse lives in the actor when he is speaking and when he is silent; the whole play must be charged with rhythm even in the pauses between words and sentences. They should all fall into the correct rhythm."

It distressed me that the brilliant scene between Orgon and Dorine in the first act didn't succeed for a long time. On his return from the country, Orgon asks Dorine what has taken place in the house during his absence. Even while listening to the details of the serious illness of his wife, he repeatedly asks:

"And what of Tartuffe?"

In spite of the most reassuring report about his favorite, each time he repeats with uneasiness and tears of tender emotion:

"Poor fellow!"

Although at times I felt deeply the humor and charm of this scene, I did not succeed in carrying it out. No matter how many variations I used in saying "And what of Tartuffe?" and "poor thing," the words did not sound alive, did not fit into the delicate tracery of Dorine's monologue; they seemed to hang in the air, heavy and false. As often happens, the scene which pleases you most of all during the reading of the play, the one on which you place all your hopes, proves the most difficult and sometimes never comes through at all. And so it was now. I didn't trust myself, I fell into despair. Everyone sympathized with me and gave me advice about how it should be played. I understood this very well, but to *act* it . . .

"Well now, what is it that disturbs you?" asked Konstantin Sergeyevich after I had helplessly blabbered this scene to him.

"I don't know what it is, but I feel that the scene is not getting anywhere. It should be witty and graceful, but when I attempt it, everything comes out dull, clumsy and uninteresting."

"Hm . . . Hm . . . I think that you don't see it right. You see the external aspects of the scene; you see its grace and you want to play that. But you must direct your images into your wife's bedroom, into Tartuffe's room; you must visualize the places about which Dorine is speaking. You are not listening to her. You must try to grasp the thoughts of your partner. Listen to what Dorine is saying: 'Your wife was sick. . . .' Just listen; no movement of either the hands or the head is necessary. But the eyes—your searching eyes—should be drawing out the news from her.

"See everything in detail.

"You are now pausing between every word. Everything that you do is in the muscles of your tongue. You don't have images. You don't really know her bedroom, but you *have* to know it, down to the smallest detail.

"Your wife is sick. In your thoughts, you should be in the bedroom where your wife is lying in a fever. It is night but nobody in the house is sleeping, everyone is rushing about. You must see this clearly. They have sent for the doctor, they bring ice; there is noise, running. . . . But right there, next to her bedroom, is the cell of Tartuffe, where he is communicating with God. They are disturbing his prayers! At once your wife is forgotten, everything in the world is forgotten, so that you may discover quickly what is happening to Tartuffe.

" 'And what of Tartuffe?'

"This is what you must train yourself to do. Don't worry

about how to say your lines, just listen attentively to Dorine and imagine what could happen to Tartuffe under such circumstances. To your question 'And what of Tartuffe?' Dorine answers: 'He ate two partridges and not much is left of the lamb.'

"My God! How that man must have worn himself out to give himself such an unusual appetite. Poor fellow!'

"As you listen to her, you make your suppositions. These are the things which are not written in the text, but as a result of which the text appears. In this lies the art of listening; the whole secret of the scene is here. Dorine, for her part, must take into consideration your reaction to each of her lines and, depending on that, say this or that. She must guess your thoughts by the look in your eyes. Besides, she is very clever and knows you very well. Therefore, in addition to the text, you must be carrying on a parallel dialogue of your own. If you combine the words of the text with your unspoken thoughts, this will emphasize the author's meaning."

DORINE:	. . . and she thanked us for everything.
ORGON	(*to himself*): Well, thank God everything is all right.
	I can imagine how happy everyone was, how they rejoiced.
	In their joy they have completely forgotten poor Tartuffe,
	Who undoubtedly restored her with his prayers.
	Probably they did not even feed him, poor man.
	And he in his humility sat by himself in his cell.
DORINE	(*to herself*): Aha!—I see, he is upset about his saint.
ORGON	(*aloud*): And what of Tartuffe?
DORINE	(*to herself*): I knew it! Well, you just watch, I'll fix you.
	(*aloud*): Knowing that she had lost a lot of strength . . . .
	(*to herself*): Aha! He is excited all right, all right.

	(aloud): He immediately restored the loss.
ORGON	*(to himself):* What, in God's name, did he do? Give his blood?
	Or what?
	(to Dorine): For God's sake, quick ...
DORINE	*(to herself):* Ah, you are interested in what kind of sacrifice he made?
	All right, if you are such a fool,
	until now you haven't understood anything ...
	(aloud): For lunch, he piously drank two extra glasses of wine.
ORGON	*(to himself):* My God! And he's not a drinking man!
	How much he loves us all! That in spite of his own health ...
	(aloud): Poor fellow.

"Naturally, this doesn't require heavy thinking or long deliberation. Thoughts flow in a moment through the heads of temperamental French people; the situation is very clear to them in all its delicacy; they understand it immediately.

"But don't forget what led up to this, what thoughts led to the speaking of the last cue. Keep in mind that a person says only ten percent of what lies in his head, ninety percent remains unspoken. On the stage, they forget this, they are concerned only with what is said aloud, and thereby destroy the living truth.

"Playing any scene, you should first create all the thoughts which precede this or that cue. You don't have to express them, but you do have to live with them. Although unspoken, the sequence of ideas conforms to that of your partner. Perhaps you might try sometimes to rehearse saying everything aloud, in order to better master your own unspoken replies and those of your partner.

"In the scene which you have just shown me, you, Orgon especially, should first of all learn to listen well in order to discover the hidden thoughts of your partner. Then those cues,

'And what of Tartuffe?' and 'poor fellow!' will find their place themselves; it is not necessary to think of them. As for Dorine, she must not forget, as she arranges Orgon's performance for Cleante, that it is being done to prove the truth of what she has just told him about Tartuffe. 'She is making fun of you,' says Cleante to Orgon after Dorine exits. Do you know what your task is, Dorine? It is to provoke Orgon so that he will behave as you want him to.

"In order to gain an accurate understanding of your behavior, rehearse not what is written, but what is meant. Let Bendina [the player of Dorine] before the beginning of each rehearsal invent some way of tricking Toporkov, so that he surely will be fooled. Then Dorine will understand what she must do in this scene with Orgon.

"You want to master the scene without preparing the way beforehand, without ordering and training your thoughts, your images; you want to grasp the result at once, to catch it from the air. It seems so simple but, you see, you didn't succeed. To be sure, it could have succeeded, but since it did not, here is a sure way to overcome the difficulties. The scene is really very difficult; remember it is a classic example of Molière's comedy."

After hearing Dorine's account of what has taken place, Orgon dismisses her and remains alone with his brother-in-law, Cleante. There is a prolonged conversation between them. Cleante at first is very cautious but gradually becomes bolder and bolder as he points out to Orgon the abnormalities in his family life which arose with the arrival of Tartuffe. Orgon assures Cleante that from the time that saintly man came to live with them the life of his family became beautiful and pious and therefore pleasing to God.

This scene is usually played in a conversational way: one character delivers a monologue and the other waits till it is over. Some speak their monologues more ardently, with more temperament, others more coldly, but it remains mere conversation, nothing more. They inevitably play this scene as dull exposition. It is unfortunate that it closes an act; dampening the ardor of an audience at the end of an act, naturally, is never advantageous for a play.

To bring this scene up, not only to the level of those violent, interesting events which precede it, but very much higher, is what our work is about.

SCENE V

CLEANTE: She makes fun of you to your face
And it serves you right, I tell you straight out.
Is it possible to fool you so easily?
Don't be angry, my dear friend—
But have you ever heard of a sedate man
Forgetting his family, himself—everything—
For a person who is far from honorable!
Be just . . .

ORGON: Wait, calm down.
You are wasting your breath;
You speak of someone you do not even know.

CLEANTE: *I* don't know? Perhaps. But in order to know him
And to form a correct opinion of him . . .

ORGON: Know! Know! I am ready to take an oath
That you will come to admire him!
What a man! Ah, what a man!
Such a man, of whom . . .
Well, in a word, a man! Of a greatness
We can never hope to reach.
Whoever follows him tastes peace of the spirit
And looks down upon the human race
With all its sad vanity. . . .
Take me: I became completely different!
My soul became closed to gentle feeling. . . .
Now if my whole family should die at my feet
I would not look at them;

           In me the smallest attachment
           To my relatives and others close to me has been
              stamped out.

CLEANTE: Completely human.

ORGON: Now, if you had met Tartuffe as I did,
           You, too, would find a friend in him.
           I noticed him at once
           When he came into our church.
           From beginning to end
           He was kneeling not far from me.
           He was praying—humbly. He was moved,
           Full of holy fire:
           He sighed, moaned and lifted his eyes
           Reverently to the sky.
           He bowed down and kissed the ground,
           And with his fist beat his breast
           As hard as he could.
           When I was going out, he rushed before me
           And with holy water was waiting for me at the door.
           Finally, I could not contain myself. . . . I decided
           To make the acquaintance of his servant.
           I started to talk to him
           And learned everything. . . . I was surprised.
           He lived like a beggar—meagerly, miserably.
           I wanted to help the poor man.
           At first he rejected it! Later, he accepted a little:
           "For me, half is too much."
           And since I wouldn't take it back,
           Before my very eyes he would give it to the beggars.
           Finally, with the blessing of God,
           He moved into my house.
           And now, as you see, little by little,
           Everything has changed in my home.
           My wife cannot evade him;
           He looks after her like a nurse.
           And if someone barely notices her, looks at her—
           That one, without hesitation—out!
           Some people call *me* jealous. . .
           But what do you think of *him?* I don't measure up to
               him.

With the slightest sin in himself,
With the simplest negligence,
He is severe, without mercy.
If in the middle of the night
It happens that while meditating, by chance he kills a flea,
Would you believe it, he cannot sleep out of remorse.

CLEANTE: My God, you have lost your mind.
Or you are playing a joke on me!
What a ridiculous monologue!
Is it possible with this blathering . . .

ORGON: Your speech is blasphemy,
It is my duty to warn you.
Listen to me: steady yourself,
It is still not too late, you know . . .
Take care!

CLEANTE: I have heard such talk before:
In your opinion, one who is blind lives righteously,
But one who can see even a little, without doubt
Is a scoundrel and a freethinker besides;
And that miserable one cannot find forgiveness.
Is this not a terrible judgement! As I don't hide
In myself bad feelings nor evil schemes
Under a mask of hypocritical grimacings,
I do not tremble for my future.

ORGON: Well! It is clear you are the only clever one . . .
Educated and learned.
Hail to you! Have it your way!
We are only donkeys and fools. . . .
Neither life's experience, nor science's wisdom
Come easily to us!

CLEANTE: Believe me, I know my value:
I am neither shy, nor do I wish to boast,
But under his pretenses I suspect trickery
And I can always distinguish a lie from the truth.
I value piety in people deeply,
In return, don't blame me if I cannot stand a hypocrite!
I cannot bear dissemblers—
Insinuating, sanctimonious, wild fanatics

And pious, shameless creatures.
Such is this fellow.
But, the brazen rascal,
Is held here in high esteem, like a rare example
Of all virtue! And he, the base liar,
Your mentor and your favorite?
Your friend and brother? Orgon, Orgon!
Consider! You are terribly blinded!

ORGON: Have you finished?
CLEANTE: Yes.

ORGON: All blessings on you.
CLEANTE: Wait a little. Let's stop this argument
And have a family talk. . . .
You have not forgotten that you gave Valere your
word?
ORGON: No, I have not forgotten.
CLEANTE: And you have fixed the day . . .
ORGON   I never forget anything.
CLEANTE: What reason is there then to postpone it?
ORGON: I don't know.
CLEANTE: Can it be that you have other plans?
ORGON: Anything is possible.
CLEANTE: To break a promise!
ORGON: I have said nothing about that.
CLEANTE: You didn't say . . . but it is vacillation,
And without cause. . . .
ORGON: It depends.
CLEANTE: Valere asked me to speak with you . . .
ORGON: Excellent.
CLEANTE: What shall I tell him?
ORGON: Whatever you wish.
CLEANTE: Now, Orgon! Why resort to such evasion
With me? You have, I see, made your decision.
Well then, why not announce it?
ORGON: My decision is not secret: to act
As my duty orders me.
CLEANTE: It means you will keep your word?
ORGON: Good-bye.

CLEANTE *(alone):* Alas, Valere, it seems
That your affairs here are not in good shape. . . .
Stand firm.

No, this is not a mere argument, not a discussion, not an academic dispute. It is a fight between two antagonists. Perhaps some kind of chance at the last moment held back the hand of Orgon from committing murder, but the blasphemous Cleante nevertheless will not escape the punishment of Heaven. As each one speaks the other does not wait complacently. Oh, no! He is like a person sitting on a burning hot stove. Each word of one grates on the nerves of the other. After this battle the two relatives become mortal enemies. This is the turning point of the play. From this moment the relationship between Orgon and his family enters a new phase; the struggle is aggravated. Orgon has come to a definite decision: He will make his only daughter, Mariane, the bride of Tartuffe. By this he will deprive his enemies of one of their allies.

We came to this conclusion after working on the scene in detail. But to formulate such tasks is not enough—you have to be able to accomplish them. How should we organize this scene? Everything we defined was still very much "in general." True, it was a fight for life or death, but what does that mean? What are the separate links in this struggle? What is the concrete task of each antagonist? What is the line of physical actions here? How can we embody all this practically? How shall we begin?

We worked under the supervision of Kedrov, who gave us very useful instructions. After we had achieved some results we went to Leontyev Lane for Stanislavski's direction. As we anticipated, Stanislavski first directed our attention to the physical behavior of the two "fighters." We presented our "sitting on a hot stove" in as many variations as possible. The whole scheme of the fight between the enraged relatives was worked out in detail, using only the words which came to us spontaneously at the time of the rehearsal. The chief thing was the physical behavior of the characters. One of us jumped up from his place and held the other pressed into an armchair (not physically, naturally, but by "inner force"). The one sitting in the armchair is like a trapped animal, ready to jump at any moment. He is waiting for the opportunity to grasp his enemy by the throat. The other, after attacking him, assumes the appearance of one who has said everything and to whom further argument is of no avail. He quietly sits down in another armchair and takes up a magazine. This enrages his opponent even more. He uses all his imagination in order to goad his opponent into action, but it is no use. The coolness of his adversary seems unaffected. But we see that, in spite of the quiet attitude of his body, just the tip of his foot is beginning to twitch. Here is his real rhythm. Suddenly the magazine flies into the far corner of the room, he jumps up as if stung, and the two antagonists, like fighting cocks, stand nose to nose.

Rehearsing the scene in such a manner, we succeeded in finding much of interest that was later incorporated into the score of the play. However, the majority of the discoveries which had helped us find the way to the successful playing of this or that scene were not used. This fight led us to more restrained, controlled forms which, surprisingly, did not weaken, but rather strengthened the inner tension.

"But, after all, Cleante finally gives up his position," objected an actor. "In all his actions there is a gradual surrender of his position."

"A weakened position *is* the result, but the *action* is 'I don't want to surrender,'" answered Konstantin Sergeyevich.

Having understood the pattern of the physical behavior of the scene, it was necessary to master Molière's text. This demanded strong creative work. The monologue of Cleante was especially difficult because the rhetoric must be overcome; and Orgon, in carrying out his passionate monologue, has to achieve the brightness and humor written by Molière.

"Work on your diction every day, every hour, not for

fifteen minutes once a week. In the diction class you speak correctly for fifteen minutes a week, but for the remaining hundred and nineteen hours and forty-five minutes in the week, incorrectly—that's nonsense. Verbal action must involve your partner in your images. To accomplish that it is necessary for you to see everything you tell him clearly and in detail. The sphere of verbal action is tremendous. It is possible to transmit thought simply by intonations, exclamations, words. The transmission of your thoughts is the action. Your thoughts, words, images—everything must be done only for your partner. But with you? Just now, Vasily Osipovich, you played the scene with your left shoulder burning the whole time because you were so conscious of the audience. This should not be. Everything should be directed toward your partner. What are you seeking to do in this scene?"

"To convince Cleante . . ."

"First, you see the expression in his eyes, then, try to change it. Strive to make Cleante's eyes show that he has understood you. What must you do to achieve this? You must transmit your images to him; it is necessary for him to see everything in your eyes. Speak not for the ear but for the eye. There can be threats, flattery, supplication—whatever you like. But everything must be only for him, for your partner. Check the results of your efforts in the expression in the eyes of your partner; don't put obstacles between you. It is true, it is inescapable, the audience is always distracting. You must be able to separate yourself from it and return to your object. In your line 'Now, if you had met Tartuffe as I did,' after the word 'now,' you pause. Why a pause? That is affected; that is for yourself, not for Cleante. What does Orgon want to express? 'Now, if you had met Tartuffe as I did, you too would find a friend in him. You would find a friend and not an enemy,' this is what Orgon wants to say. So why then make a senseless pause after the word 'now?' You just invented something to color the sentence and you are listening to yourself because you want to know if it sounds well. Never prepare for

a word or an action; otherwise, you will have self-conscious-
ness in place of intuition. But we *must* prepare our attention
with that creative 'toilette,' about which I have spoken. We
must express the thought as a whole. Whether it sounds convincing or not, only your partner may judge. You verify
according to the expression of his eyes whether you have
achieved your aim. If not, invent other ways, set in motion
other images, other colors. The only judge of whether what I
am doing on the stage is correct or incorrect is my partner. I
myself cannot judge this. The most important thing while
working on a role is to develop images in yourself. You say:
'Now, if you had met Tartuffe as I did,' but do you yourself
remember exactly how you met him? Can you tell me in detail
about that—the location of the church where you first saw
Tartuffe in prayer, the interior of the church, etc.; in short,
everything which made such an impression on you? Unless you
see all that, you won't be able to find the action, the color and
the temperament needed to convince Cleante. Your actions
appear convincing, correct and organic only when your images are concrete and detailed. Otherwise, they will not convince the audience.

"In order to develop in yourself that feeling of rapture,
that naïve love Orgon has for Tartuffe, with which he is
possessed, it is not necessary to become agitated and force
your feelings. It is impossible to inspire oneself by using forced
feelings. Create the whole history of this love; don't omit any
detail of it. Your fantasy must work here. The whole history
should be filled with interesting events, touching details. The
very thought of Tartuffe should arouse in you images enriched
by all the best human qualities which exist. Create in your
imagination the image of such an unusual man. To do this it is
necessary for you to see him clearly, very clearly. Perhaps
there is someone who exists, or who existed, among people you
know whom you worship—Leo Tolstoy, perhaps, or someone
else. When you create this history, draw the image of that
saintly person in your imagination. Then try to make your

partner see him. And don't spare the colors; change them boldly, let them be unexpected. This defines the rhythm of the scene. If it does not work out, it means that you, Toporkov, are not seeing what you should. You must change your images of Tartuffe, because the Tartuffe whom you now see is either *very* small or not dear enough to you. Therefore, it appears that there is nothing worth talking about. Remember that with Molière as with Gogol there is no moment without 'heat.' That means that if you want to convey how Tartuffe was praying, you have to put all your temperament, all your fire, into the telling.

"Consider the story about the flea:

'. . . by chance he kills a flea,

Would you believe it, he cannot sleep out of remorse.'

"Do you see that picture clearly, this sign of the great goodness and benevolence of Tartuffe? Do you see how he jumped out of bed at night, naked, shivering from the cold; how he lighted the lamp, told his servant about the 'misfortune' which had occurred, how they both looked for the flea for a long time, how Tartuffe, finding it, warmed it with his breath, trying to bring it back to life, how he later put it on a clean piece of paper and prayed the whole night, crying bitterly. This kind of picture, or something like it, must arise in your inner vision when you try to arouse a feeling of reverence in Cleante toward the saintly Tartuffe.

"Again and again I repeat: all this is *only* for Cleante. Stir him either by horror or by tears, whichever is more comfortable for you. If one thing does not work, try another color, another adaptation, but do not think about your intonations. We should not deliver one sentence at a time, we must draw the whole picture. Don't break up the statue of Venus and show her piece by piece; show her as a whole. The public distracts the actor from creativity. You must fascinate your partner by your will, rhythm and bright images. It is terrible when an actor's will is weak. Direct all your effort toward changing Cleante's attitude toward Tartuffe. Playing with the partner is like a chess game. You cannot anticipate all the moves; you can only watch the voice, the intonation, the look and the movements of each muscle of your partner. According to them, you determine how you should proceed. Then it will be genuine acting.

"Remember, Orgon is taking great pains and Cleante is listening attentively. After finishing his story about the flea, Orgon is sure that he has turned the godless Cleante to the path of truth and looks at him in triumph. But Cleante simply says, 'You have lost your mind.' Do you appreciate what this means to Orgon? In this lies the comedy of Molière. We must play this scene every time as if for the first time; bring nothing of the former methods of acting to which you were attached. Otherwise, your playing becomes stereotyped instead of what I ask you for: live, organic action each time. Just remember your tasks: Each person in the scene is convinced that he is right and wishes by any means to immediately bring the other to terms; each one wants that passionately. So solve this task today, right here, right now. Transmit to each other your own images. One sees in Tartuffe a saintly person who sheds tears over a dead flea; the other sees a rogue who plans to destroy the whole family. Because of this, you jab at each other."

Working on this scene, Konstantin Sergeyevich at first focused on the line of physical actions, then gave his attention to the text. He forced us to repeat many times now this, now that sentence in order to master phonetic clarity. Although making sure that our images were fully developed, he returned constantly to the line of physical actions.

"Here your purpose is to convince. Is this action psychological or physical?"

Or, turning to Cleante:

"It disgusts you to listen to Orgon, but that is not action, it is a condition. What is the physical *action* here? In the first place, it is possible 'not to listen'; that is your simple physical action. To pretend to be cold-blooded is also an action. How will you do this? There are a thousand different possibilities, but they cannot be thought out beforehand. It is most important to be able to encourage or to reject. At first do what a person usually does who listens to another with interest, and then do the opposite. What will your behavior be if your task is to discredit all that which comes from your partner, if your action is not to listen, to appear cold-blooded? Your behavior is a tuning fork for the behavior of your partner."

We did what Konstantin Sergeyevich advised. I spoke the same monologue to different reactions from Cleante: once he listened to me attentively, quietly encouraging me to a further opening of my spirit; another time, on the contrary, he discredited my fiery speech by yawning and becoming more deeply interested in a magazine which was lying on the table, then by whistling a joyous little song. In another variation Cleante seemed at any moment ready to interrupt me and burst out into a thundering speech. We employed all these actions, now one, now another. These exercises no doubt benefited us. Being obliged all the time to check on Cleante, I completely forgot that Stanislavski's eyes were on me. I felt better, my self-confidence returned. My actions arose spontaneously, especially in those moments when I had to regain Cleante's attention or prevent him from interrupting me. Many bright, unexpected colors and intonations appeared.

However, Stanislavski still was not satisfied with them and demanded a greater and greater variety of colors and adjustments.

"Keep in mind that human adjustments to situations and people and the means of expressing one's feelings are innumerable and almost never straightforward; enthusiasm, for example, is not always communicated by 'enthusiasm' but often by something completely different. It is possible to say 'How wonderfully this actor is playing!' with admiration, with indignation, with contempt, with rapture . . . even with tender emotion."

Stanislavski demonstrated these variations to us very convincingly. He made me repeat that part of the monologue

where I express my strong admiration for Tartuffe in these
many different ways. But all this had to be done with an
expression of rapture.

> "... I am ready to take an oath
> That you will come to admire him.
> What a man! ... Ah, what a man!
> Such a man, of whom ...
> Well, in a word, a man! Of such greatness
> We can never hope to reach."

Sometimes, saying the first two lines with rapture, I received the command from Stanislavski: "With indignation!"
So I changed the color. Then he gave the order: "With despair!" And I changed to despair.

This scene interested Stanislavski very much. We worked
on it persistently for a long time because he considered it good
material for technical exercises.

Konstantin Sergeyevich sorted out all the elements of his
system while working with us. After one of these showings
Stanislavski gave special attention to "moments of communion."

"What is wrong today? There is communion at moments
but you lose it, and furthermore your objects are too 'heavy'
for a French play."

Stanislavski regretted that the actors often ignored this
communion, this important living process, that they did not
study it, did not understand its smallest links and especially its
most important and essential element—that orientation which
precedes action not only in man but in animals as well.

He often said to us, "Pay attention to how a dog comes
into a room. What does it do first of all? After it comes in, it
sniffs the air to determine where its master is, it approaches
him, gets his attention and, only after it has achieved this,
enters into 'conversation' with him. A man behaves in exactly
the same way, only with much more subtlety and variety.

"What does an actor do? He comes on the stage according to the mise en scène, goes where he is supposed to and immediately enters into conversation with others, not troubling to find out whether they are disposed to listen to him or not. Place before him a man instead of a woman and he won't notice; he will declare his love to the man. Without the correct orientation, the organic living process is destroyed. The actor begins to lie; he doesn't believe in his actions and descends to hackneyed playing. Only by observing all the laws and subtleties of behavior can the actor achieve a feeling of truth on the stage and use the creativity of his organic nature.

"Of what elements does communion consist? 1) Orientation, 2) searching for the object, 3) getting the attention of your partner, 4) making contact with your partner, 5) creating images and making your partner see them as if with your eyes, 6) thinking only of the images, never of the intonations of the words, and 7) considering how best to transfer these images and events to your partner.

"You have just played a scene of an argument between two enraged people, but you started the argument immediately, leaving out a very important element which should have preceded it—the orientation, that is, making contact with each other, adjusting to one another, establishing 'radio waves.' Paying attention to this makes it easier to begin your talk. These subtleties, these little physical actions, although established before the argument begins, are developed further with the first five or ten lines and are the beginning of the chain of the through-line-of-action of the given scene. If you leave them out, you destroy the truth.

"A person comes to another to ask a favor. But before he approaches the heart of the matter, even before he says the first word, he senses his chance of success, and the other can often guess his purpose. That is the result of their quick feeling out of each other, of their orientation, of their attentive observation of each other's action and behavior.

"After a mutual exchange of compliments, and after having adapted themselves to the circumstances and the atmosphere of the moment, they get to the heart of the matter.

"All these psychological subtleties invariably are present in one's dealings with other people. They must never be ignored in our art; they are decisive for us. They convince both the actor and the audience of the genuineness, the authenticity, the truth of all that is taking place on the stage. They are a very important part of the technique of embodiment.

"You must begin with mutual contact, then develop your quarrel to the very highest point until you finish with a complete break. Only such a development compels the audience to follow your battle with unwavering attention and forces it to maintain the tension right up to its conclusion. If the elementary logic is broken, the audience will stop believing you. If it becomes indifferent, you can regain its attention only by returning to the observance of the smallest details of the logic of human behavior.

"We cannot rely merely on 'presence' on the stage; we must work on our art, our speech, our acting. Once onstage, the first sentence spoken must serve as a tuning fork. By your fourth or fifth sentence, you must recognize where you are acting and where you are overacting; where you are just relying on your 'stage presence' and where you really are living. Then it is necessary to establish live contact with your partner. So! But we must also establish correct breathing and voice quality.

"The actor must be able to determine what is good and what is bad in his performance. He must do this quietly and without agitation or confusion. What do you need on the stage? Attention plus sensitivity to and concentration on the given circumstances. These are the necessary conditions for the creative feeling to arise in the actor. It will be present if you believe in what you are doing and do it truthfully. With the help of these qualities, the 'I am' emerges.

"There are theatres where they love falsehood, where they cultivate it. There are others which fear the false. I say to you: Do not fear the false, it is a tuning fork for the truth. You

should not cultivate it, but it is not necessary to fear it. I never
had a single role where I did not start with clichés. When I
felt perfectly comfortable in a part and thought that I was
playing like a god, I was actually playing according to clichés.

"Often the actor tries at all costs to act well, but this is
impractical, impossible. It is necessary to go on the stage not
to *play* something but to *act*, to conquer. We cannot play
calmness; there must be truth in our calmness. We cannot
play a feeling, a passion or an action 'in general,' we must act
truly, properly. The less the effort, the greater the effect on
the audience. What does it mean 'to try harder?' It means
flirting with the public—making the audience the object. This
is one of the actor's greatest temptations. Far better than
flirting with the public is not to notice it at all."

Turning again from the question of acting technique,
Konstantin Sergeyevich paid special attention to giving definition to the separate scenes. He showed how to deepen the
interpretation of a play by concentration on its idea, its images, its essence.

"We must avoid the usually accepted way of playing Molière, the way which transforms Molière's living people into
boring stereotypes, mere masks. That is awful; it is always
tiresome and unconvincing. There is a convention that comedy must be played in that way. Instead, you must believe in
what is happening on the stage and place yourself in the midst
of it. Drama, comedy, tragedy do not exist for the actor. There
is only *I*, a person in the given circumstances. Consider what
has taken place: Rasputin has settled in the home of Orgon
and disrupted the life of the family. The objective of the
action of the play, the objective of everyone in the play except
Orgon and his mother, is to free themselves from Tartuffe/
Rasputin. Orgon and his mother, on the contrary, settle Tartuffe in the bosom of the family and submit completely to his
will. This is what the bitter fights in the play revolve around,
but the actions of each are in logical sequence and each one
fights in his characteristic manner.

"Remember, on the stage a loud cry may not indicate

strength but weakness. Intensity of the voice comes as a result
of fascination with intuitively found motivation. When properly arrived at, this gives birth to correct adaptations and
colors.

"The player of the role of Orgon does not have to think of
the comic side of the role. In the course of events the humor
and comedy play themselves. For Orgon all that happens is
pure tragedy. If you think about it thoroughly and put yourself
in his place, your reasoning will be approximately this: 'I have
met a person through whom I may directly communicate with
God himself. I believe this in all sincerity. I want happiness for
my whole family, which I love very much. I want to create a
happy, beautiful life for them. I have brought a genuinely
saintly person into my home. This is my greatest achievement.
This is the turning point toward a bright future, and this is so
evident that only a blind man could not see it.' Suddenly not
only is this not accepted as a divine gift, but a vile persecution
is carried on against that messenger of God: they try blas-
phemously to defame him, to put him out of the house.

"Acting with all sincerity, Orgon strives to reason with his
relatives in order to save their souls from Divine punishment.
He breaks with his wife and his brother-in-law, throws his son
out of the house and disowns him. Finally, crouched under a
table, by his own eyes and ears he is suddenly convinced of his
near-fatal mistake. He has given refuge in his home, not, let us
say, to Tolstoy or Jesus Christ, but to a real scoundrel. Isn't
this a tragedy?

"The climax of the play occurs in the scene when Orgon
comes out from under the table, where he has overheard
Tartuffe's loving talk with his wife, and says the famous line:
'He's a perfect monster. I admit it!'

"Usually the actor who plays Orgon tries at this moment to
call from the audience Homeric laughter. If you, Vasily Osipovich, succeed here in evoking not laughter but sincere
sympathy for yourself—that will be your triumph! Consider
carefully the deep meaning of the play; do not look at the

events in the play with the eyes of an actor but with those of a human being. Put yourself in Orgon's place. You really love your wife, your daughter and son and the others in the play; understand how hard it is for you to see them going to their destruction, and what it would mean to you to break all relations with them. What must be the strength of your faith in the holiness of Tartuffe if, despite this, you nevertheless persist in your steadfastness. You want to have Tartuffe's approbation. To win the esteem of a simple man is one thing, but to obtain that of Christ—that is something completely different. From this springs your pathos. It is completely justified here, especially when 'Christ' wants to leave your house. Do you comprehend what this would mean to a religious man? If you evaluate all this correctly, in the end you will understand. Do you appreciate now how this will nourish your temperament, how it will bring you to great depths of pathos as you defend Orgon? Here is true Shakespearean passion. Above all, you must understand the tragedy of Orgon. The comic element arises of itself through the disparity, the incongruity between your behavior and what is really taking place in the house. The humor of your position will come; don't worry about that, worry about other things. Live through his tragedy and through that you will come to high comedy. Here is the stubbornness not of a fool, but of a man who is defending the best, the holiest in his life, the very light of his life itself. The more you are inspired with these thoughts, these images, the more you will enrich the role and the sharper, more relentlessly will the vile vice of hypocrisy be branded. This is the seed of Molière's play and the aim of our production, its superobjective.

"Each member of the audience must see himself in Orgon. He will laugh heartily at those situations into which he fell because of his misplaced trust and his imprudence; in other places he will blame himself or be indignant at the vileness of people who live parasitically on the weakness of those close to them. He may even drop a tear, but the play, nevertheless, still will be a comedy. The audience will receive a sharp sting, but it will go out of the theatre enriched.

"But do not try to achieve everything at once. That is not in your power, you will strain yourself. Rehearse one thing at a time, follow the path to the climax while strengthening the line of physical action, developing and enriching your images.

"It is possible to play everything as a foolish anecdote, but what will be the result of such a performance? Will that satisfy a discriminating audience? Is it worthwhile to work for that in the theatre? Each of our performances must carry an idea. In addition to acting and carrying out the fundamental through-line-of-action, you must always keep in mind the superobjective of the play.

"I remember once when we went on a guest tour to Petersburg that before the opening of the engagement, we rehearsed many times in the theatre in which we were going to play. Sometimes the rehearsals lasted till two or three o'clock in the morning. One time, tired after our work, I came out of the theatre in order to go to the hotel to rest and was astounded by the spectacle which confronted me. On the street was a heavy frost; in the darkness of the night the lights of bonfires appeared in several places and the whole square was filled with people. Some were warming themselves at the bonfires, rubbing their hands, legs, ears; others were standing in groups, arguing spiritedly. Smoke from the bonfires arose, the crowd murmured in a thousand voices. What was this? 'These people are waiting for tickets for your production,' I thought. 'My God, what a responsibility we have to satisfy the spiritual needs of these people who have been standing here freezing all night; what great ideas and thoughts we must bring to them!'

"So consider well, whether we have the right to settle accounts with them by merely telling them a funny anecdote. I could not fall asleep that night for a long time because of my feeling of responsibility. The idea came to me that in addition to the superobjective of the production, there should be a *super*-superobjective. I could not yet define it, but that night I felt that the people whom I had seen in the square deserved much more than we had prepared for them."

CONCERNING OUTER CHARACTERISTICS

NOT ONE OF THE elements of artistic technique was neglected by Stanislavski in his work with us. In the first period of the work all our attention was concentrated exclusively on physical actions; later, thoroughly, persistently, the other parts of stage action were forged: the words, rhythms, ideas, images, the reading of the verses, etc.

I would like to say in conclusion some words about one of the most important elements in our technique of embodiment—the outer characteristics. In my descriptions of our rehearsals I have touched lightly upon this point, but it would be a mistake to think that Stanislavski gave secondary importance to this aspect.

Himself a marvelous character actor, most skillful in embodiment, he naturally wanted to lead his pupils to a similar mastery, but, as always, he had his own special ways.

Considering the fact that there is no difference between the art of the stage and the art of emotional experience, that is, the art of embodiment, Konstantin Sergeyevich refused to let us play *feelings,* we must always play *images.* "It is necessary to play the *character,*" he said. "Of course, you cannot act without feeling, but it isn't worthwhile to worry and fret about it. It will come of itself as a result of your concentration on live action in the given circumstances.

"As for the outer characteristics, they appear as a result of a deep penetration into the inner world of the character.

202

These special outer characteristics will be more easily found by the actor when the logical line of the behavior of the character has been assimilated, has become his own. The outer characterization completes the work of the actor. Premature worry about these outer characteristics leads the actor to imitation and may prove a hindrance to his finding living, organic behavior."

Did Stanislavski, then, advise the actor to repeat himself in each role, to use his customary methods and thus bring the role down to the level of his own limitations? Definitely not! After deciding what must be done in order to accomplish the task of the embodiment of the through-line-of-action of the character, the actor begins his researches with himself, with his own natural qualities, gradually developing them and striving to bring them to the heights demanded by the play or by the imagination of the creators of the production, the actors and directors.

Konstantin Sergeyevich tried by every possible means to keep us from the cheap methods of creating outer characteristics which were still used in some theatres, methods that hide a living face under a mask of clichés—lisping, stammering, changing the natural voice, adjusting the pince-nez on the nose to indicate a doctor, twisting the mustache for a colonel, etc.; in short, all those things which permit the actor to cling to the easiest, the usual way of expressing the character. This path leads him not to the expression of the character as a whole but only to the expression of the outer shell, that is, to *playing* the outer characterization. Konstantin Sergeyevich considered this disturbing to the organic development of the living stage character, capable of immobilizing it completely.

As the actor discovers and follows the logical line of behavior of the character, his line of physical actions, involuntarily and, possibly, unnoticed by himself, he finds the features of his outer characteristics. This is inevitable. No matter how hard a good actor tries at the start to avoid visualizing the appearance of the character in order to concentrate on its inner essence, the outer image will still arise in his imagination from time to time. There is nothing to fear in this. Everything which comes without forcing while working on the part should be accepted with gratitude by the actor.

Konstantin Sergeyevich found his own particular ways to divert the actor from following the path of outer imitation.

Once Konstantin Sergeyevich spoke with me on the telephone after seeing a dress rehearsal of V. V. Stanitzin's production of Dickens' *The Pickwick Club* in which I was playing Pickwick's servant.

"Everything in your outer characterization is very good: you are young, very adroit, you move beautifully, but you still do not know why you need all these qualities. Adroitness for the sake of adroitness belongs in the circus. Your actions are not definite, they are not united by a single aim. They are somewhat contradictory. Some of them are absolutely unnecessary. Your inner character which would unite all your motives and actions, which would give you belief in your actions, is not yet developed."

"And what could the essence of this role be, Konstantin Sergeyevich?"

"One must think about it; it is difficult to say at once. Could it be to look after Pickwick? If so, try to subordinate all your behavior to this one aim: to look after him. Choose what is necessary to carry out this aim, and throw away the rest without regret, no matter how good it seems to you. Then the character will acquire purposeful activity in accordance with the inner line. As for the outer characteristics, if you just make him adroit and agile, well, he might as well be an acrobat or a monkey or something of that sort."

One of the greatest actors of the Russian theatre, Davydov, in his conversations with students, always repeated over and over again:

"First it is necessary to find the trunk of the part, then its main branches, then the much smaller twigs, later the shoots and leaves, and finally the veins on the leaves."

Stanislavski also used to speak of the creation of the character in definite steps: first, the strengthening and mastery of the through-line-of-action of the part; after this, all the rest, including the outer design. Naturally, each of the elements of the role brings about the others. Having built the scheme of physical actions, which is the very first step of the work, the actor is on his way to discover the outer characterization. One is not possible without the other, but he should not think about it at the start. Konstantin Sergeyevich kept to a careful, gradual development and, while helping the actor to examine logically every detail, tried not to overload him with tasks beyond his strength. When the moment came to transfer attention to the outer characterization, Konstantin Sergeyevich spoke about it directly:

"What is a fat man? How does his behavior differ from that of a thin man? The body of a stout man always leans slightly backward, his feet spread apart. Why does this happen? The center of gravity of a stout man is shifted to the stomach, and this makes him lean backward to maintain his balance. His plump, fat thighs do not permit his legs to move as they do in a normal person. The change in his walk comes from this."

Stanislavski then asked an actor to walk into the room with his legs apart and to imagine increased weight in his stomach. He tried to have the actor bring this characterization gradually to every part of his role until he had mastered it, had strengthened this new quality until it became habitual, living and organic for him. The audience must believe in his great weight even without quilted padding. Then when the actor puts on padding, the audience will not notice it and the actor will not feel it strange.

"What about an old man? Above all, his joints are badly bent. He can neither sit down nor get up without leaning on something. This is what you have to master. The logical behavior of a drunken man is not that he staggers but that he tries *not* to stagger. Try to find out how to do this."

Analyzing each detail of the role's outer characteristics in this way, Konstantin Sergeyevich showed us exercises by which we could express them. One will recall the exercise with a drop of mercury that he showed me when I had trouble with Chichikov's bow in *Dead Souls*.

But is this the only way to approach a part? May not the actor, while reading his part, at once see its outer image with its definite, characteristic details and begin immediately to embody those features? May he not come to the same result, that is, the full mastery of the character in all its complex qualities? Such a possibility is certainly not ruled out. Stanislavski himself speaks of this in *My Life in Art*. But, his many years of directing and acting showed Stanislavski that the way from inner to outer is more dependable and more truly reflects the spiritual side of the human character than merely copying its outer characteristics. To doubt the effectiveness of this procedure is to question Stanislavski's whole system. We must not forget that Stanislavski himself referred to his system as a means to be used "when the part doesn't come easily." However, if an actor achieves success by working with another method or without any method at all, you can look upon him as an exception. Let those "masters" work as they will.

Even when I followed Stanislavski's path gropingly, stumblingly, I always felt it close to my actor's temperament, my individuality. Any deviation from this way invariably brought failure and disappointment.

THE FIRST SHOWING OF TARTUFFE TO THE LEADERS OF THE MOSCOW ART THEATRE

With Stanislavski's death in 1938, the "orphaned" actors who had worked with him on *Tartuffe* found themselves in an awkward position: to continue the experimental work without the leadership of Konstantin Sergeyevich did not seem possible ... but to stop the work seemed a pity. The only resolution to the problem appeared to be to stage a production. But the directors of the theatre did not have any idea how ready the material was; we ourselves could not tell. The work of Konstantin Sergeyevich differed so from the usually accepted norm that it was difficult to know if we were close to that point when we might transfer the play to the stage.

We knew that we had worked hard, that we were achieving some success here and there, that we were mastering both the play and our roles. We could play separate scenes, perhaps, but we had no way of judging whether they were good or bad. We had become so accustomed to them that we had lost the "taste." Each of us could only guess whether he was playing his part in the ensemble according to the "score"

worked out with Stanislavski during our rehearsals. Not all the
scenes had been rehearsed. We had not once played through a
whole act, and we had not even touched the last act. Our
mood was far from optimistic.

The management of the Theatre decided to look at the
material we had worked on and then, together with the directors, determine the fate of the production.

We were given a place to rehearse; then we had to decide
on one or two acts to show Sakhnovsky, who represented the
Theatre's artistic management. From that moment our group
came to life again. The name of Molière's play appeared in
the rehearsal schedule and we became utterly absorbed in our
work. Now it took on a more "practical" character. We had to
tie together pieces which had been worked out separately; we
had to take off the scaffolding of our construction in order to
show a small part of the future "building." We worked with
enthusiasm; we wanted to do everything possible not to disgrace our teacher.

We came to the demonstration, not having any idea
whether we would succeed or fail. Kedrov, now the leader of
our group, admonished us not to try too hard, not to "act"
anything.

"No 'feelings,' no 'temperament,' just check your actions,"
he said.

The demonstration exceeded our expectations.

The very first moments, when nobody "acted" anything
but just tried to make the necessary adjustments, aroused the
sharpest attention of those present, and this couldn't help
being reflected in the feelings of the actors. All of us achieved
a high level of attention, of concentration. It turned out that
everything which had become habitual and commonplace for
us, the technique which we had mastered without realizing it,
appeared fresh and spontaneous to those watching the
rehearsal. It aroused their interest, riveted their attention, and
as *our* concentration grew, as the events of the play captivated
us, each member of the audience became absorbed with the

headlong struggle in the house of Orgon. The sequence and logic of our actions gave us that faith which reveals temperament. We became unrecognizable as actors; the talent of each opened in a new, unusual quality, like a sudden flowering. All this was the result of the laborious, persistent work of Stanislavski and Kedrov over a long period. At the time we had not understood what fruit this work would bear. Observing the work of my companions now, I was amazed how effortlessly, how naturally they went from one task to another, fulfilling each clearly and convincingly, as if no difficulties, doubts, or sweating of blood had ever occurred at the rehearsals. I cannot say anything about my own performance except that in the scene with Cleante, where I try to convince him of the holiness of Tartuffe, I understood for the first time all the sense, all the deep meaning of that which Stanislavski called "images." I remember very well that for the first time I visualized clearly my meeting with Tartuffe, how he was praying in the church, how he cried about the flea and what his appearance was. In me arose a passionate wish to convey all this to Cleante clearly and at great length. It was annoying that he would not understand. This was evident by the expression in his eyes, by the impatient movement of his shoulders, by the skeptical, wry way the corners of his mouth were drawn down, ready at any moment to change into a sarcastic smile, etc. Not the slightest counteraction of his escaped my attention. I read all his thoughts and each of them poured oil on the fire for me. When Gerot said at the end of the scene that for the first time he saw my eyes unusually alive and expressive, I understood that he, too, had come to recognize the importance of this. We realized that in this rehearsal each of us had overcome difficulties which the day before had seemed insuperable.

The demonstration was a triumph for us: opinions about us changed radically; conversation in the lobby took another direction. The artistic leader of the Theatre, Sakhnovsky, had a long conversation with the directors next day. In addition to

Sakhnovsky, Kedrov, Bogoyavlenskaya and I also took part. The "new quality" of our acting surprised Sakhnovsky. He said:

"I never thought that it would be possible to play Molière so that the life onstage would be so convincing. But with you, each character came into the room, not from backstage, but on some business definitely important for him, something concerning him very much. Everyone was joined together with thousands of threads. I believed that Elmire really *was* the wife of Orgon, and Mariane his daughter, not simply actresses who were playing these roles. In short, I believed to the very end. I believed that it was genuine life. I understood the passion with which the members of the family were fighting to save their hearth; I sympathized with them. I could not follow the development of this conflict indifferently, and every second I was ready to take part in it myself, notwithstanding the fact that I know the play almost by heart. This so excited me, so startled me! You completely spared me the traditional cliché performance of Molière, which until now has been usual on stages all over the world. In your production you did not separate the life of the characters from your own. Wonderful! You brought your real, live feelings and your emotional experiences onstage and completely discarded the worn-out clothes of the clichés. I am only afraid that they may creep into your performance later on when you put on the costumes and wigs."

It is impossible to say what satisfaction his words gave us. It meant that, to some degree, we had reached that quality toward which Stanislavski had led us. It remained for us not to lose what had been acquired, but to develop it in order to attain the fullest embodiment of the play.

Kedrov took upon himself the carrying out of this task and strove to resolve the many new problems which arose in connection with the change in the aim of our work. If the previous period was one of work on perfecting acting technique, on the reeducation of the actor, on the achievement of a new method for the actor to use in working on himself, now, on the foundation that had been laid, the finished stage production had to be created. Now came the synthesis of all the elements of theatre. The play was not an invention of funny masks but of great passions, a comedy of exceptionally sharp situations, where the tension of each person was brought to the highest point. We wanted *Tartuffe* to become again the living, passionate, contemporary play it had been three hundred years before, when it was written. We wanted to show that in our day, as then, exposing hypocrisy would help put an end to sanctimoniousness.

Tartuffe opened on the fourth of December 1939. On the posters and programs of the play this epigraph appeared:

"This work, begun under his artistic leadership,
is dedicated to the memory of
the People's Artist K. S. Stanislavski"

In connection with the work on *Tartuffe*, Kedrov said:

"Creating the performance, we were working according to the "method of physical actions." What is the essence of this method? Konstantin Sergeyevich used to say that when we say 'physical actions' we are fooling the actor. They are *psycho*physical actions, but we call them physical in order to avoid unnecessary philosophizing. As for physical actions, they are concrete and easily understood. Precision of action—concreteness in its fulfillment in a given performance—this is the foundation of our art. If I know the exact action and its logic, then it becomes for me a score; how I carry out the action according to the score here, before *this* audience—that is creativity."

Stanislavski and Kedrov, who finished the work, created a performance where the human theme was heard. In the past Molière was "represented." Performance was given for the sake of performance, where trick gave rise to trick for the sake of "theatricality" and shone with the cold light of fireworks.

This vulgarity disappeared at the Moscow Art Theatre where human beings and the truth of human life took its place. This, it seems to me, was the essence of the Moscow Art Theatre productions.

The performances had a great success with the audiences. The critics also treated them very favorably, and it was gratifying to us that the special quality we had striven to attain was noted by them.

One thing was apparent to all who participated in this production of *Tartuffe*—the presence of a creative atmosphere that existed both onstage and backstage. I do not speak only of the actors, but of the technical personnel as well; they knew the meaning of this production and responded wholeheartedly.

We all felt the invisible presence of Stanislavski, and the desire of each one of us not to disgrace his memory became our super-superobjective.

CONCLUSION

"THE MORE I OCCUPY myself with questions about our art," Stanislavski once said, "the shorter my definition of high art becomes. If you ask me how I define it, I will answer: it is that in which there exists a superobjective and a through-line-of-action. Bad art is that in which there is neither superobjective nor through-line-of-action."

Stanislavski could not conceive of the embodiment of a character by means of cold, mediocre hackwork. He dreamed of an artistic technique which could deal with genuine human feelings, emotions, passions.

"To play a part means to transfer to the stage the life of the human spirit," said Stanislavski. But is it possible to create the life of the human spirit without having created the genuine flow of life on the stage? The very fact that what is taking place on the stage is organic does not necessarily create stage art, but, by selecting the necessary and discarding everything unnecessary, the actor or the director gives conviction to the flow of scenic life and, in that way, creates art. The more organic its material, the higher its quality will be and the closer it will be to an authentic portrayal of life.

Not satisfied with the state of contemporary acting technique, Konstantin Sergeyevich often said: "Our art is still a dilettante art, because we do not have a genuine theory; we do not know its rules, we do not even know the elements of which it is composed. Take, for example, music. Its theory is very exact, and the musician has at his disposal everything

213

needed to develop his technique. At his service are innumerable exercises, etudes, for the training of all the qualities which are demanded by his art: dexterity of fingers, a sense of rhythm, a good ear, mastery of the bow, etc. He knows that the foundation of his art is *sound*. He knows very well the sounds of the scales with which he has to work. In short, he knows what he must do to reach perfection. We cannot name a single violinist who doesn't practice four or five hours every day. And so it is in all the other arts. Show me even one actor who does anything toward perfecting his mastery outside of rehearsals and performances. Such a one cannot exist for the simple reason that he would not even know how to begin. We do not know the elements of our art. We do not know the 'scales,' we do not have either etudes or exercises, we do not know what we have to train, what we have to develop. Most surprising of all, this disturbs few of us. It is said, on the contrary, that in this lies the unusual charm of our art, not in some kind of inconvenient theory which smacks of mathematics; no, we have Apollo to aid us."

Observing the work of great actors, Stanislavski strove, first of all, to discover what special quality made their acting great. He tried to understand by what means they achieved this, what method they used in working on a part, what their creative process was. After defining the elements of the actor's art, he wanted to create a technique by which the ordinary actor through faithful, daily training could overcome his limitations and perfect his acting technique to the point where it could be called "artistic" technique.

Stanislavski worked constantly to overcome the actor's inhibitions which prevent him from expressing his creative nature.

In working out any moment in a scene in a merely craftsmanlike way, one may use ten methods, but nature has innumberable methods. Therefore, do not force, just act according to nature's rules. This is the only true way: Persistent work on yourself until you reach a truly artistic technique which will bring you into agreement with nature. The way to organic creativity lies through truth and belief in what you are doing. In order to encourage our organic nature to work with our subconscious, we must create a normal flow of life on the stage.

It is difficult to conceive of the development of a theory or technique of any art until the elements of which it is composed are known and clearly manifested. Who will deny that in music there is sound; in painting, color; in drawing, line; in pantomime, gesture; that in literature and poetry there are words? But in our art? Ask a group of workers in the theatre and each will answer differently and their answers will not, as a rule, be that which was already known a thousand years ago as undeniable truth: *Action* is the chief element of our art— "genuine, organic, productive, expedient action," as Stanislavski so often insisted.

The stage character expresses first the action of a human being. The actor is called upon to embody the living actions of a person as set forth by the author. After reading over the episodes of the play, the actor defines for himself the logic of the separate links of the unbroken line of conflict. This is the beginning of the work on a part. The "tasks," "the through-line-of-action," "the seed" of the role—these won't be discovered at once. Ultimately, they appear as the result of searching for means of carrying out what finally prove to be the simplest tasks, tasks which should have been completely obvious at the beginning. Going from one episode to another, the actor gradually clarifies for himself the whole line of his behavior, of his conflict, of his logic during the entire course of the play. This line must never be broken. It starts for the actor far in advance of the beginning of the play; it finishes for him long after its end. It must not be interrupted in the moments of his absence from the stage. Its embodiment must be accurate, clear and completely truthful. A person who in life desires to gain the confidence of those around him is obliged never to break the logic and sequence of his deeds, but to be scrupulously truthful in carrying them out.

The effectiveness of the actor is based upon these same

rules. This is the most correct, the naturally correct way. The embodiment of any action demands the mobilization of all elements of the person's behavior. In life this proceeds from within as the natural reaction to this or that event, but on the stage all the events are imaginary, fictitious, incapable of calling forth a "natural" reaction. How then can the actor arrive at the embodiment of the organic line of behavior of the stage character?

Konstantin Sergeyevich directed our attention to what is the most tangible, the most concrete in each human action: its physical aspect. Especially in his last years, he gave the greatest importance to this aspect of the life of the role, beginning his work on a character with it. Diverting the attention of the actor from "feelings," from psychology, he directed it toward the carrying out of purely physical actions. In this way the actor could penetrate in a natural way into the sphere of feelings.

"Build the simplest possible scheme of the physical actions of the role," he said. "Follow the line of these uninterrupted actions, and you will have already achieved at least thirty-five percent of the role."

The scheme of physical actions is the frame on which everything that makes up the essence of the human character is built. It reflects most expressively all the feelings, all the emotional experiences included in the stage character in the most convincing way.

That mastery of our art toward which Stanislavski urged us seldom comes easily. It must be achieved by hard, persistent daily work over the course of one's whole life. To think of oneself as standing in the ranks of those geniuses to whom everything is given as a gift from Heaven is a delusion; geniuses appear rarely. Make it clear to yourself once and for all that our art is very difficult and that we must overcome this difficulty with persistence. Unfortunately, because acting seems very simple and easy, there are few who really understand this. The better and more perfect the playing of an actor, the easier, the simpler seems his art.

The actor who can achieve the highest technique and mastery of the creation of a human character will occupy that honorable place reserved for the genuine artist. The audience, responding to his art, is grateful to him for moments of noble emotion which it carries home and relives for a long time. For such an artist, no one can ever feel anything but deep respect, and everyone will recognize the power of his art on the spirit.

In order to create truth on the stage, it is necessary to develop in oneself an ability to sense it. It is the same as a musical ear in a musician. This quality is to some degree inborn, but it can be developed. Truth and organic behavior on the stage demand from the actor continuous, unabated work on himself in the course of all his activity; they demand an attentive study of life, a wholehearted awareness of the life around him. The subtle nuances out of which human relationships are formed are often expressed in hardly noticeable physical actions; they must be studied thoroughly by the actor and used in his daily exercises. Onstage we must become consciously aware of all that which in life we perform easily and instinctively. This must be practiced until it becomes unconscious and habitual onstage.

Some of our leading theatre workers and critics have branded Stanislavski's technique mere "mathematics" or "mechanics." This has come about because the new technique has been mastered by very few and is not perfectly clear to others. Learning it presents great difficulties, but directors and actors through whom the ideas of an author are carried out cannot neglect any possibility for the development of their technique, no matter how complicated it may seem to them in the beginning.

A dramatic production, which is in essence a reflection of human life, is much more convincing when it embodies living, organic action. The ability to create a genuine, living character is peculiar to the art of the actor, but the creation of a living, human character demands, I repeat, especially great skill and mastery, a special technique completely different from that hackwork which is often substituted for art. These two techniques differ from each other as much as the cultivation of living plants differs from the manufacture of artificial flowers.

Not infrequently, actors who are not considered artists, who indeed have rather a bad reputation, are, nevertheless, for some reason thought to possess the technique of their profession. It is said of such an actor: "Yes, he has bad taste, he is crude, but he has a rich technique." The technique which gives rise to a crude, tasteless form of acting is not that technique of which we are speaking. The ability to impress an audience with cheap effects—to throw comic or sentimental lines in order to get applause, to make ostentatious entrances and exits, to "milk" the audience at the end of the performance, to upstage one's partner, to drown out his speeches or to use them to draw attention to oneself—is no more than the skill of a hack. Such actors can be crude, as we have said, or more subtle when a more demanding audience sees their work, but, their work cannot be regarded as artistic technique and, therefore, does not interest us.

The creation of a living, *really* living person—this is the goal of high art. The artist who succeeds even once in identifying himself with the stage character he has created is aware that he has accomplished a very great thing and experiences deep happiness. This doesn't happen often, but the actor who has once achieved this is forever after dissatisfied with any substitute for true creativity, even though audiences may have praised his lesser achievements. Only when the events of the play have been assimilated into his own mind and the actor genuinely starts to live the life of that other being created by his imagination, when the logic of that being has become *his* logic and his actions come in response to the subtlest emotional experiences of the character—only then does he know the joy of the master who has created a genuine work of art.

Based on the traditions of the Russian theatre, Stanislavski in his study of the techniques of directing and acting achieved results unprecedented in the history of theatre art. His was an invaluable service to art and we are justly proud of this distinguished genius of our country.

BIOGRAPHICAL NOTES

BELI, ANDREA (1880–1934), the pseudonym for Boris Nikolaye-vich Bugayev, a leading poet, symbolistic writer and literary critic.

BELINSKY, VISSARIAN GRIGOREVICH (1811–48), the first represen-tative of the non-aristocratic intelligentsia, a critic, and one of the leaders of Westernism. He originated the sociological school of liter-ary criticism which prevailed until the end of the nineteenth century and which has been revived by the Communists.

CHERNISHEVSKY, NIKOLAI GAVRILOVICH(1828–89), a university professor and literary critic, leader of the radical intelligentsia dur-ing the 1850s and sixties. His famous liberal novel, *What Is To Be Done?* aroused university students all over Russia because of its revolutionary ideas and inspired a stirring students' song. Its im-mense popularity contributed to his nineteen years' banishment in Siberia.

CHUSHKIN, NIKOLAI NIKOLAYEVICH (1906–77), an authority on the art of the Moscow Art Theatre and an advocate of the heritage of Stanislavski and Nemirovich-Danchenko. He worked at the Stan-islavski Museum and prepared its works for publication; he was editor and author of a series of introductory articles in the collected works of Stanislavski and author of books and articles dedicated to the Moscow Art Theatre, its actors, directors and designers.

DALMATOV, VASILY PANTELEYEMONOVICH (1852–1912), a famous artist of the Alexandrinsky Theatre, has been called "the dandy of the Russian stage."

DAVYDOV, VLADIMIR NIKOLAYEVICH (1849–1925), a greatly rev-ered teacher at the Imperial Theatre School in Petersburg and a leading actor of the Alexandrinsky Theatre. He was well known for his realistic portrayals of characters in the plays of the Russian classical dramatists.

DMITRIEV, VLADIMIR VLADIMIROVICH (1900–1948), a well-known scenic designer for theatre, opera and ballet.

GOGOL, NIKOLAI VASILYEVICH (1809–52), is regarded as the father of the realistic school of the Russian theatre. He urged the creation of Russian plays "reflecting the life of Russian society and the character of Russian men." Like Shchepkin, he emphasized the importance of the ensemble and required the actor to identify with the character "so that the thought and aspirations of the impersonated character be appropriated by the actor himself and that these stay in his mind during the entire performance." A great friend of Shchepkin; it is often questioned which had the greater influence on the other.

GORCHAKOV, NIKOLAI MIKHAILOVICH (1898–1958), a talented director under Vakhtangov at the Third Studio, worked under Stanislavski for many years and became a leading Soviet director until his death in 1958. He wrote *Stanislavski Directs*, a detailed account of Stanislavski's application of his system in rehearsals with the new young members of the Moscow Art Theatre.

KACHALOV, VASILY IVANOVICH (1875–1948), came to the Moscow Art Theatre in 1900. He acted Trigorin in *The Sea Gull* and many other leading roles. He has been called the most versatile actor in the company.

KATAEV, VALENTIN PETROVICH (1897–   ), two of whose plays, *The Embezzlers* and *Squaring the Circle*, represented a new trend toward "satirical and gay comedy without artificial morality."

KHMELOV, NIKOLAI PAVLOVICH (1901–45), entered the Moscow Art Theatre in 1924 and, after the death of Nemirovich-Danchenko in 1943, was appointed its artistic director.

KNIPPER-CHEKHOVA, OLGA (1870–1959), was one of the original company of the Moscow Art Theatre and considered its greatest actress. She played Masha to Stanislavski's Vershinin in *The Three Sisters*. She married Anton Chekhov in 1901.

KORENEVA, LYDIA MIKHAILOVNA (1885–   ), a leading actress of the Moscow Art Theatre. Among the productions in which she appeared were *Tsar Fyodor, Uncle Vanya, The Brothers Karamazov, An Enemy of the People, Tartuffe* and, in 1952, *The Queen of Spades*.

LEONIDOV, LEONID MIRONOVICH (1873–1941), along with Knipper-Chekhova, Kachalov and Moskvin, has been called one of the actors of the Moscow Art Theatre who best made clear the quality of naturalness in its most complete and inclusive sense. He played the title role in Stanislavski's production of *Othello* and won praise during the American tour of 1923 for his acting in *The Cherry Orchard*.

"LILINA" (PEREVOSHCHIKOVA, MARIA PETROVNA) (1866–1943), the affectionate name given to Stanislavski's wife. She was one of the founders of the Moscow Art Theatre and one of its principal actresses. Her playing of Masha in its first production of *The Seagull* contributed to its extraordinary reception.

MICHURINA-SAMOILOVA, VERA VASILEYEVNA (1824-1880), wwitth her husband, Vasily, among the leaders of the new style of realist acting initiated by Shchepkin.

MOSKVIN, IVAN MIKHAILOVICH (1874–1946), played Ivan in the Moscow Art Theatre's production of *The Ardent Heart*. He was a leading actor of the Moscow Art Theatre. One of its original members, he played the role of Tsar Fyodor in its opening production. He especially pleased Chekhov with his playing of Epikhodov in *The Cherry Orchard*.

NEMIROVICH-DANCHENKO, VLADIMIR IVANOVICH (1858–1943), co-founder of the Moscow Art Theatre. An author in his own right (he was twice awarded the Griboedov prize), Danchenko was to have the final word in literary matters and Stanislavski, the final word in matters concerning the artistic form of production.

PUSHKIN, ALEXANDER (1799-1837), has been called "the founder of the Russian literary language and the father of the new Russian literature." To reform Russian playwriting, he urged that Shakespeare be taken as a model. He is best known for his novel in verse, *Eugene Onegin* (1823–31), and for *Boris Godunov* (1825) and *The Queen of Spades* (1854). All three are familiar to us as operas. Stanislavski considered Pushkin's requirement for the playwright: "truth of passions, genuineness of feelings in given circumstances" as a basic requirement for an actor. Pushkin was a friend and admirer of Shchepkin.

SAVINA, MARIA GAVRILOVNA (1854–1915), the "uncrowned queen" of the Alexandrinsky Theatre and Turgenev's "last love".

SHCHEPKIN, MIKHAIL SEMYONOVICH (1788–1863), is said to be the founder of the realistic school of acting on the Russian stage. He discovered for himself a natural tone of voice discarding the old manner of declamation; he worked meticulously on a role to give a characterization a realistic foundation admonishing the actor to "get into the skin of the character." His superior acting on the estate where he was a serf and in provincial theatres inspired his admirers to raise enough money to buy freedom for him and his family in 1821 when he was thirty-four years old. For the next forty years he played at the Moscow Imperial Dramatic Theatre, the Maly (Small) Theatre which became known as the Home of Shchepkin.

SIMOV, VIKTOR ANDREYEVICH (1858–1935), a very talented scene designer, engaged for the production of Hauptmann's *The Sunken Bell* by the Society of Art and Literature. He was retained when the Moscow Art Theatre was formed, designing its first production, *Tsar Fyodor.*

STEPANOVA, ANGELINA OSIPOVNA (1905–   ), came to the Moscow Art Theatre as a young actress from the Third Studio of Vakhtangov when it was decided that the theatre needed new blood. Stanislavski worked very intensively with the young actors from both the Second and Third Studios. He considered Stepanova a very gifted actress and his opinion was justified as she became one of the principal actresses of the Moscow Art Theatre.

STRELSKAYA, VARVARA VASILEYEVNA (1838–1915)   spent all her artistic life at the Alexandrinsky Theatre where she won acclaim for her portrayal of Lisa in Griboedov's *Woe from Wit.*

STREPTOVA, POLINA ANTIPEYEVNA (1850–1903), an important actress at the Alexandrinsky Theatre, she was well known for her portrayal of Ostrovsky characters.

TOPORKOV, VASILY OSIPOVICH was born in Petersburg in 1889 and died in Moscow in 1970. *Stanislavski in Rehearsal* was written in 1949–50. In 1964, he came to the United States at the invitation of the State Department along with Angelina Stepanova, a leading actress of the Moscow Art Theatre, Vladimir Prokofiev, its historian, and Victor Manucov, teacher at the Moscow Art Theatre School. They offered a seminar to specially invited theatre people.

VARLAMOV, KONSTANTIN ALEXANDROVICH (1848–1915), famous for his portrayal of comic characters. Was one of the leading players at the Alexandrinsky Theatre in Petersburg.

YERMOLOVA, MARIA NIKOLAYEVNA (1853–1928), the greatest actress of the Russian theatre, star of the Maly Theatre, "pride of the

Russian stage," she was considered by Stanislavski to be the greatest actress he had ever known, not excepting Duse. She was outstanding in Schiller's *Maid of Orleans* and *Mary Stuart,* and played Phèdre and Lady Macbeth.

ZUEVA, ANASTASIA PLATONOVNA (1896–), came to the Moscow Art Theatre early and remained with it until her retirement. She was a very gifted character actress and was well known for her portrayal of the part of Korobochka in *Dead Souls,* which she played in the Theatre's visit to New York in 1965.